D1453755

ON THE HAPPY LIFE

ON THE
HAPPY LIFE
ST. AUGUSTINE'S
CASSICIACUM DIALOGUES,
VOLUME 2

Translation, Annotation, and Commentary by
Michael P. Foley

Yale
UNIVERSITY
PRESS
New Haven & London

Published with assistance from the foundation established in memory of
Philip Hamilton McMillan of the Class of 1894, Yale College.

Yale University Press books may be purchased in quantity for educational,
business, or promotional use. For information, please e-mail sales.press@yale.
edu (U.S. office) or sales@yaleup.co.uk (U.K. office).

Set in Electra type by IDS Infotech, Ltd.
Printed in the United States of America.

Library of Congress Control Number: 2018961529
ISBN 978-0-300-23852-5 (hardcover : alk. paper)
ISBN 978-0-300-23858-7 (paper : alk. paper)

A catalogue record for this book is available from the British Library.

This paper meets the requirements of ANSI/NISO Z39.48–1992
(Permanence of Paper).

10 9 8 7 6 5 4 3 2 1

In grateful memory of
Fathers Ernest L. Fortin, A.A., and Matthew L. Lamb,
inspiring teachers who sparked, fanned, and guided
my love of these dialogues.

Noverim me, noverim te.
May I know myself, may I know Thee.

—*Soliloquies* 2.1.1

CONTENTS

PREFACE

My goal in translating the four Cassiciacum dialogues of St. Augustine is to introduce the serious English-speaking student to an extraordinary tetralogy that is relatively underestimated and prone to misappropriation. Accordingly, this translation aspires to be as literal as is reasonable.

A literal translation, in which Latin words are given their closest approximation in English and in which the same English words are generally used for their Latin equivalent, suffers from several drawbacks. First, it is cumbersome. Trained in rhetoric, Augustine chose words not only for their meaning, but for their resonance; unfortunately, any mellifluence or connotations that go with that resonance are compromised in translation. Second, it is disconcerting. Certain styles or conventions popular in Augustine's time, such as the earthiness adorning even the most sublime of passages, are no longer in favor. Nowadays, for instance, grown men do not generally speak of fleeing to the nursing bosom of Lady Philosophy (see *Against the Academics* 1.1.4). Third, an absolutely consistent literal translation is impossible when translating a language with fewer than sixteen thousand words into one with more than thirty times that number. Latin's modest vocabulary encourages an author working in that language to use one word several different ways whereas an English author is freer to use a different word each time. To translate, then, the same Latin word with the same English word in every instance can be misleading, and it clanks against the Anglophonic ear. But not to translate certain terms consistently, despite its oddity in English, would be to forgo perhaps vital clues the author has left in his text—for a language's apparent weaknesses can turn out to be hidden strengths in the hands of the right wordsmith.

In an attempt to overcome these difficulties, I adopted the following strategy. First, I allowed the goal of a literal translation to be trumped by the canons of good prosody when the literal meaning was virtually nonsensical and when a freer translation posed no threat to understanding the intellectual content of the work. When Augustine says in *Against the Academics,* "Don't look . . . for something that is difficult to find anywhere among the peoples (*gentium*)," he is using a classical figure of speech, where *gentium* means "on earth" (1.2.6); hence, it is translated accordingly. Second, when I do depart significantly from the literal sense of the text, I acknowledge it in the Notes so that the reader may retain some access to the original wording. And third, I employ a Translation Key. When a significant Latin term can be translated several different ways, I note its variants; and when there is only one English word for two different Latin words, I designate one of the English words with an asterisk (*) and pair it with only one of the Latin words to distinguish it from the other (here I am inspired by Hippocrates Apostle's translations of Aristotle). Augustine, for instance, uses both *animus* and *anima* for the soul, and so the former appears as "soul" and the latter as "soul*." Both the annotation and the Translation Key, incidentally, are intended for readers making a close study of the text who may not be proficient in Latin.

If, however, these aids become a distraction from reading and enjoying the dialogues, readers should ignore them. Tools that are not helpful should be placed back into the box.

Yet despite the aforementioned drawbacks and the extra effort that must be made to overcome them, a literal translation remains advantageous for one simple reason: it alone liberates readers from what has been called the tyranny of the translator. Animated by the commendable goal of easy comprehension, translators are often tempted to paraphrase loosely in order to make the meaning of texts more digestible or palatable to a contemporary audience. Such translations, it is claimed, save readers from the disorientation that would ensue from an unmediated encounter with an alien worldview. Free translations of this sort constitute a kind of well-intentioned paternalism.

There is a thin line, however, between being paternalistic and being patronizing, and translators who do not faithfully reproduce a text into another language unwittingly take a condescending attitude, it seems to me, both to the authors they are translating and to the readers for whom they are translating: to authors, because their ideas are implicitly treated as inferior to those that are currently popular; and to readers, because it is assumed that they have neither the desire nor the capacity to wrestle with the work as originally crafted.

The antidote to this condescension, as a twentieth-century political philosopher once noted, is for the translator to "conceive of himself as a medium between a master whose depths he has not plumbed and an audience of potential students of that master who may be much better endowed than is the translator." This model works well for translating the writings of St. Augustine. As Augustine himself reminds us in *On the Teacher*, in order to know the meanings of words, we must first know the realities to which they point;

and as he discusses in *On Christian Doctrine,* both the mode of ascertaining meaning and the mode of communicating it once it is ascertained are difficult to carry out. Some of the realities to which Augustine points are indeed difficult to grasp, especially in dialogues that, he stresses, deal with a subject only the rarest type of human being can comprehend (see *On Order* 1.1.1). It therefore behooves translators of Augustine to approach their task with special care and humility, even a sense of unworthiness.

Humility is an important quality for readers as well. Rather than approach these ancient texts as possibly interesting monuments to a quaint or benighted chapter in world history, I earnestly recommend that we read them as if our very lives depended on them, as if they were our only chance of escaping the shadowy cave into which historical happenstance or our own short-sightedness has placed us. I do so from the conviction that a great book offers the hope of freeing us of the prejudices that from our earliest days we have sucked up like mother's milk or into which our dissolute living has placed us (see Cicero, *Tusculan Disputations* 3.1.2). What we learn might not, in the final analysis, be any less fallible than our own opinions, but the only way we will know for certain is if we let authors speak for themselves, listening with one sincere assumption: that they have something worthwhile to say. Perhaps then and only then will we be able to graduate from milk to meat.

ACKNOWLEDGMENTS

I wish to thank the Ernest L. Fortin Foundation, the Baylor University Summer Sabbatical Program, and the Summer Stipends Program of the National Endowment for the Humanities, all of which provided generous material support for this four-volume project in 2006–2007, 2005 and 2007, and 2010, respectively; Dr. David White in the Baylor Classics Department for his meticulous and *extensive* corrections and improvement of these translations; Drs. Matthew Walz of the University of Dallas and Douglas Kries of Gonzaga University for their invaluable feedback; Dr. Gerard Wegemer and the participants of the 2011 summer seminar titled "Augustine's and More's Use of Cicero in the Cassiciacum Dialogues, *City of God, Utopia* 1," sponsored by the Center for Thomas More Studies at the University of Dallas; Jennifer Banks, Susan Laity, Heather Gold, Jessie Dolch, and the rest of the expert team at Yale University Press; Dr. Ryan Womack and Alexandra Foley for their patient proofreading; and my students who conjured up the spirit of Cassiciacum in the Baylor University seminar courses on these dialogues in 2007, 2008, and 2011.

TRANSLATION KEY

The following table shows the translations of several key terms in Augustine's early dialogues, first in English-Latin and then in Latin-English. Exceptions to the rules given here are mentioned in the annotation of each work. As mentioned in the Preface, when there is only one English word for two different Latin words, I designate one of the English words with an asterisk and pair it with only one of the Latin words to contradistinguish it from the other.

English	Latin
to approve	In Academic thought, when assent to something as true is impossible, the wise man may approve (*approbare*) of certain things as plausible or probable so that he may have a ground for action (see *Against the Academics* 2.5.12).
to assent	The wise man, according to Academic skepticism, should give his assent (*assentiri*) only to that which he absolutely knows to be true (see *Against the Academics* 2.5.11–12).

to know   Augustine uses several Latin verbs for "knowing" or "becoming acquainted with," such as *noscere, cognoscere,* and *novisse.* These usually refer to a knowledge of passing, temporal things, but sometimes, because they are fairly generic terms, they can also be used to designate knowledge of the highest and eternal things.

to know*   *Scire* is the verb that is generally, though not always, used to designate the highest and most secure kind of knowing (see *On the Happy Life* 2.7, *Soliloquies* 2.1.1).

knowledge   *Cognitio* is most often a generic term for knowledge.

knowledge*   *Scientia* usually refers to the highest kind of knowledge, that is, the grasp of eternal realities such as the truths disclosed in the liberal arts. See *On the Immortality of the Soul* 1.1: "All that the soul knows (*scit*), it has within itself; nor does knowledge (*scientia*) contain anything other than that which pertains to some discipline, for discipline is the knowledge (*scientia*) of anything whatsoever" (see also *Against the Academics* 1.7.19).

measure   *Modus,* which is also translated as "limit," is a key concept in the dialogues, especially in *On Order.* In *On the Happy Life* 4.34, Augustine describes God the Father, the First Person of the Trinity, as the *summus modus* or "Supreme Measure."

mind   *Animus* is also translated as "soul" or even "heart," depending on context (see *Against the Academics* 2.2.3 and entry for *animus* below).

mind*   *Mens,* along with reason (*ratio*), is defined by Augustine as the ruling part of the soul (*animus*) (see *Against the Academics* 1.2.5). In *Soliloquies* 1.6.13 it is characterized as the "senses" or "eyes" of the soul (*anima*), while reason (*ratio*) is the "looking" of the soul and understanding (*intellectus*) is the "seeing" of the soul.

opinion
: In some respects the antithesis of knowledge or *scientia*, opinion is that from which the philosopher, especially the Academic skeptic, wishes to be free (see *opinio* below).

to perceive
: *Percipere* is usually used in reference to basic sensory activities rather than higher acts of understanding. It can, however, designate comprehension of an intelligible reality, as when one "perceives" the truth or falsehood of a definition (see *Against the Academics* 3.9.21).

probable
: *Probabile*, mostly translated as "probable," is associated with the Academic doctrine of probability or plausibility (see *probabile* below).

to sense
: *Sentire* is usually used in reference to either bodily sensation or the mental awareness and use of the bodily senses. It is usually translated as "to sense" or "to feel," though context sometimes compels other variations, such as "to judge" at *Against the Academics* 1.3.8.

sense, sensation, etc.
: *Sensus* is translated, depending on context, as "senses," "sensation," or "sense-perception." *Sensus* can refer either to the five bodily senses of sight, sound, touch, taste, and smell *or* the mental faculty that enables people to use their senses for seeing, hearing, touching, tasting, and smelling (see *Against the Academics* 1.1.3, *Soliloquies* 2.2.3); in one case, Augustine uses *sensus* for the capacity to understand (*On the Happy Life* 4.25). Augustine regrets that he did not differentiate between physical and mental *sensus* by adding "bodily" to the former kind (see *Retractations* 1.1.2; *Soliloquies* 1.6.12, 2.2.3).

soul
: *Animus* is also translated as "mind" or even "heart," depending on context (see *Against the Academics* 2.2.3; see also entry for *animus* below). *Animus* is used only for human, that is, rational, souls.

soul*   *Anima* is that which gives life to the body or flesh (see *Confessions* 10.7.11). All plants and animals as well as humans have *anima* or this principle of life (see *Soliloquies* 1.2.7). One of Augustine's goals in the *Soliloquies* is to prove that the *anima* of a human being is immortal.

understanding   *Intellectus* is also sometimes translated as "intellect." In *Soliloquies* 1.6.13, *intellectus* is defined as the "seeing" (*visio*) of the soul (*anima*), while mind (*mens*) is the "senses" or "eyes" of the soul and reason (*ratio*) the "looking" of the soul. In *On the Immortality of the Soul* 6.10, *intellectus* is similarly defined as the "seeing" of the soul (*animus*). In *Against the Academics* 3.19.42, the Second Person of the Trinity, God the Son, is the Divine Understanding.

verisimilar   *Verisimile* is also translated as "similar to the true" or "like the true." It is a technical term employed by the Academic skeptics, reputed to be synonymous with "plausible" or "probable" (see *Against the Academics* 2.5.12).

Latin	English
anima	"Soul*" is that which gives life to the body or flesh (see *Confessions* 10.7.11). All plants and animals as well as humans have *anima* or this principle of life (see *Soliloquies* 1.2.7). One of Augustine's goals in the *Soliloquies* is to prove that the *anima* of a human being is immortal.
animus	"Mind," "soul," or even "heart" (see *Against the Academics* 2.2.3), depending on the context. In *On the Immortality of the Soul*, Augustine writes that in humans, reason is either *animus* or in *animus* (2.2) and that when we reason, it is *animus* that is doing it (1.1). The best or "ruling" part of *animus* in humans is mind (*mens*) or reason (*ratio*) (see *Against the Academics* 1.2.5). In the *Confessions* Augustine

writes that to *anima* belongs sensation as well as the interior sense that correlates sensory data and of which *animus* makes use (10.6.10–10.7.11).

approbare, To "approve" or "give approval." In Academic thought,
approbatio when assent to something as true is impossible, the wise man may approve of certain things as plausible or probable so that he may have a ground for action (see *Against the Academics* 2.5.12).

assentiri, To "assent" or "give assent." The wise man, according to
assensio Academic skepticism, should give his assent only to that which he absolutely knows to be true (see *Against the Academics* 2.5.11–12).

cognitio Most often, a generic term for knowledge.

comprehendo To "comprehend" or "grasp," either by the senses or by the mind (depending on context). According to the Stoics, when a mind truly comprehends something, it has such a clear impression of it that it is completely different in every way from a false impression. This gives rise to an irresistible conviction in the knower's mind that the impression is true (see *Against the Academics* 2.5.11).

fallor "To be mistaken" or "to be deceived," depending on context. In the *Soliloquies*, Reason defines *fallax* as something that is deliberately deceitful rather than merely untrue or fictitious (2.9.16), but this definition is not adhered to throughout the dialogues as a whole.

intellectus "Understanding," "the understanding," or, sometimes, the "intellect." In *Soliloquies* 1.6.13, *intellectus* is defined as the "seeing" (*visio*) of the soul* (*anima*), while mind (*mens*) is the "senses" or "eyes" of the soul and reason (*ratio*) is the "looking" of the soul. In *On the Immortality of the Soul*

6.10, *intellectus* is similarly defined as the "seeing" of the soul (*animus*). In *Against the Academics* 3.19.42, the Second Person of the Trinity, God the Son, is the Divine Understanding.

mens "Mind*," along with reason (*ratio*), is defined by Augustine as the ruling part of the soul (*animus*) (*Against the Academics* 1.2.5). In *Soliloquies* 1.6.13 *mens* is characterized as the "senses" or "eyes" of the soul (*anima*), while reason (*ratio*) is the "looking" of the soul and understanding (*intellectus*) is the "seeing" of the soul.

modus "Measure" or "limit" is a key concept in the dialogues, especially in *On Order*. In *On the Happy Life* 4.34, Augustine describes God the Father, the First Person of the Trinity, as the *summus modus* or "Supreme Measure."

noscere, "To know," either as a knowledge of passing, temporal
cognoscere, things or as a more generic term for knowing that could
novisse include knowledge of the highest and eternal things.

opinari, opinatio, "To form an opinion" or "to opine," "forming an opinion,"
opinio, opinator "opinion," "opiner," respectively. A technical term in Academic thought, an opinion should never be formed by the wise man, although he may hold various positions or make decisions on the basis of things that he approves as plausible or probable. In the Cassiciacum dialogues, the Latin phrase *ut opinor* (in my opinion) is fairly common and may not have a technical connotation.

percipere "To perceive," usually used in reference to basic sensory activities rather than higher acts of understanding. It can, however, designate comprehension of an intelligible reality, as when one perceives the truth or falsehood of a definition (see *Against the Academics* 3.9.21).

probabile	A critical term for the Academics in their defense against the Stoic charge of *apraxia*, namely, that their skepticism leads to inactivity. In Academic thought, *probabile* signifies something that is "plausible," "persuasive," or "approvable" rather than something that is certainly true to which one can give full assent. It is allegedly synonymous with "verisimilar." *Probabile* is mostly translated as "probable," but it should not be confused with the modern notion of probability as a form of statistical likelihood.
scientia	"Knowledge*" usually refers to the highest kind of knowledge possible, that is, the grasp of eternal realities such as the truths disclosed in the liberal arts. See *On the Immortality of the Soul* 1.1: "All that the soul knows (*scit*), it has within itself; nor does knowledge (*scientia*) contain anything other than that which pertains to some discipline, for discipline is the knowledge (*scientia*) of anything whatsoever" (see also *Against the Academics* 1.7.19).
scire	"To know*." *Scire* is the verb that is generally, though not always, used to designate the highest or most secure kind of knowing (see *On the Happy Life* 2.7; *Soliloquies* 2.1.1).
sensus	*Sensus* can refer to either the five bodily senses of sight, sound, touch, taste, and smell *or* the mental faculty that enables people to use their senses for seeing, hearing, touching, tasting, and smelling (see *Against the Academics* 1.1.3; *Soliloquies* 2.2.3). In one case, Augustine uses *sensus* for the capacity to understand (*On the Happy Life* 4.25). He regrets that he did not differentiate between physical and mental *sensus* by adding "bodily" to the former kind (see *Retractations* 1.1.2; *Soliloquies* 1.6.12, 2.2.3).
sententia	Most often, a "position" (a stance in thought or debate), but also a "notion," "statement," "viewpoint," and "decision" (especially an official juridical decision).

sentire

Usually, "to sense" or "to feel," though context sometimes compels other variations. It is used in reference to either bodily sensation or the mental awareness and use of the bodily senses.

verisimile

"Verisimilar," "similar to the true," or "like the true." It is a technical term employed by the Academics, reputed to be synonymous with "plausible" or "probable" (see *Against the Academics* 2.5.12).

visum, videri

Visum is the past particle of *videre* (to see). It sometimes takes on the technical meaning of an "impression" in Stoic epistemology and is translated as such (see *Against the Academics* 3.9.18). The verb *videri* is translated as "seems" or "appears" and has to do with the realm of appearances or percepts that are not necessarily real or true.

GENERAL INTRODUCTION TO THE CASSICIACUM DIALOGUES

AUGUSTINE AT CASSICIACUM

In the autumn of A.D. 386, St. Augustine retired to the country villa of his wealthy friend Verecundus, located somewhere north of Milan in a place called Cassiciacum. He had brought with him several of his acquaintances and loved ones: his friend Alypius, his mother Monica, his illegitimate son Adeodatus, his brother Navigius, his cousins Lartidianus and Rusticus, and two spirited pupils named Licentius and Trygetius. There, Augustine not only recovered from the chest pains that had compelled his recent resignation as a teacher of rhetoric, but he began to reflect more deeply on the faith he had come to accept as true. The conversations held during this time of "fruitful leisure," interrupted occasionally by farm work and violent poultry, were allegedly preserved with the help of stenographers who were hired largely for practical reasons: to spare Augustine's health by reducing his need to speak and to provide a record for those who were not present. Later, Augustine edited the transcriptions with the help of his co-retreatant Alypius. Rather than preserving the discussions verbatim or arranging them chronologically, the two friends fashioned dialogues along pedagogical and thematic lines. The result of these labors is the tetralogy of *Against the Academics*, *On the Happy Life*, *On Order*, and the *Soliloquies*.[1]

What was Augustine hoping to achieve at Verecundus's villa? Certainly, he was preparing for his baptism and initiation into the Catholic Church, which would take place in Milan the following Holy Saturday on April 24–25, 387. Augustine had converted to Christianity in the late summer of 386, an event that he vividly recounts in book eight of the *Confessions*; but his actual reception into the Church would take time. One of the interesting aspects, then, about the Cassiciacum dialogues is that they were written by a mere catechumen, a candidate for baptism. Because of the early Church's so-called *disciplina arcani*, or "discipline of the secret," being a catechumen in the late fourth century meant not experiencing all of the Church's practices and teachings. Augustine the catechumen may have engaged in advanced theological speculation at Cassiciacum, but he probably did not know the wording to the Apostles' Creed, which was taught to catechumens only a few weeks before their baptism. And he may have known that the Eucharist was the bread of life, but he had probably never seen the Eucharist, since catechumens were dismissed from Mass after the homily.[2] On the other hand, Augustine profited much from listening to the sermons of St. Ambrose, from his socializing with the intellectual elite of Christian Milan (such as Manlius Theodorus, to whom he dedicates *On the Happy Life*), and from his own studies. Consequently, even though he was not yet a Christian layman, Augustine was well equipped for his first written venture into what is now sometimes called philosophical theology.

But more than prepare for his own baptism, Augustine wanted to lead others to the same breakthroughs that had brought him to where he was. This aspiration is evident in his solicitude for his students Licentius and Trygetius, as well as in his appeals to Romanianus and Zenobius, the two friends to whom he dedicates *Against the Academics* and *On Order*, respectively. It is not difficult to infer that Augustine is also eager to assist his readers in the same way.

Those breakthroughs of Augustine's, as I have called them, are more aptly described as a "conversion," or turning around, and following the narrative order of the *Confessions*, they may be roughly identified as belonging to one of three kinds.[3] In book seven of the *Confessions*, Augustine describes an "intellectual" conversion that was instigated by a reading of the Platonists; in book eight, he recounts a "moral" conversion that finally freed him from his addiction to the pleasures of the flesh; and in book nine, he touches upon a "religious" conversion that formally "bound" him to God in baptism and enabled him to experience, together with his mother Monica, the so-called Vision of Ostia.

The *Confessions* was written two decades after the Cassiciacum corpus, but the same three kinds of conversion are present in Augustine's early thought and can therefore serve as a useful reference point for interpreting the dialogues. The most conspicuous of the three at Cassiciacum is intellectual conversion, the cognitional revolution whereby one is able to differentiate between sensible and intelligible reality, that is, between that which can be grasped by any of the five bodily senses and that which is grasped by the mind or intellect alone. Contrary to our daily commonsensical assumptions that privilege the tangible, visible, audible, olfactible, and gustable, the intellectually converted mind recognizes that the reality of physical things is caused by something that is not physical but can be grasped only by our intelligence, far removed from the senses and even from physical images of any kind. This revolution in thinking, which ascends from sensible data to realities not intrinsically conditioned by space, time, or matter, is crucial because it alone enables one to understand, however dimly, the two things that Augustine identifies in the *Soliloquies* as most worth knowing: God and the soul.

Moreover, intellectual conversion is made possible by a special "return to ourselves" whereby we recognize our own minds and our own desire to know as intelligible rather than sensible realities.[4] Erik Kenyon identifies this return to oneself as the not-so-hidden agenda unifying all of Augustine's dialogues: behind every "first-order debate" about a topic (skepticism, happiness, theodicy, etc.) is a "second order" that consists of an "inquiry into inquiry." The Cassiciacum dialogues, Kenyon goes so far as to argue, "look foremost" not to a set of answers about first-order issues but "to the act of inquiry itself: The fact that we can inquire at all tells us various things about ourselves. By reflecting on our own act of inquiry, we are put in a position to improve how we go about inquiring" because reflection on our inquiry yields a discovery of "cognitive norms of thought" operative in "most if not all acts of rational inquiry." Such a discovery clears the mind of errors such as materialism and serves as a guide for further investigation.[5] The liberal arts, which come up frequently at Cassiciacum, are instrumental in these purging breakthroughs because their aim, according to Augustine, is to point to eternal, intelligible realities and to canons of reason that competently direct human inquiry.

Yet although intellectual conversion through a return to oneself is crucial to grasping reality as it truly is, such a conversion is an insufficient condition for acting responsibly and justly. "And what did it profit me when I read and understood all the books of the arts which they call liberal," Augustine asks in the *Confessions*, "while I remained the vile slave of evil desires?" Besides a conversion of one's intellect or understanding, a conversion of one's behavior or mores needs to occur that enables one not only to know the good but to do the good, to feel and act in a way that is consistent with what is right. It is Augustine's concern for moral conversion at Cassiciacum that explains his attentiveness to "the order for living," his advice to his pupils on how to live well, and his sharp criticism of them when they fail to do so. It also explains why Reason, Augustine's mysterious interlocutor in the *Soliloquies*, probes Augustine's heart with embarrassing questions designed to gauge whether he has suffered any moral relapses.[6]

Moral conversion begins the life of ethical excellence and makes one fit to have the best kind of friendships. That said, neither intellectual nor moral conversion satisfies the deepest yearnings of the human mind and heart. Something more is needed, both as a completion and grounding of these conversions and in order to bring the human person to ultimate happiness. Hence the need for religious conversion, which in biblical terms is the replacement of one's heart of stone with a heart of flesh (see Ezek 36:26) that enables one to love the Lord God with one's whole heart, whole soul, and whole strength (see Deut 6:4–5). Religious conversion is a surrender to divine love. It is "religious" in its modern meaning as ordered toward a formal and communal worship of God, but it is also "religious" in its ancient meaning as a binding (*religio*) of the soul to God. For Augustine, both senses are operative in the sacrament of baptism; and for Augustine, such a binding in the Christian religion does not involve a restriction but an expansion of one's freedom as well as a perfection or completion of the other two conversions, for in addition to knowing the good and doing the good, the individual is now capable of fully loving the good. "Without doubt," Monica concludes in the second dialogue, "this is the happy life, the life that is perfect. And we must presume that we who are hurrying to it can be brought to it by a firm faith, a lively hope, and an ardent charity."[7]

By being attentive to Augustine's overarching goal at Cassiciacum of intellectually, morally, and religiously converting his audience, readers can better appreciate the various twists and turns that the dialogues take. And these three kinds of conversions can even act as a gauge for the similarities and differences between the *Confessions* and the writings from Cassiciacum. Rather than trace Augustine's alleged move away from Neoplatonism to orthodox Christianity as many have tried, it may be more fruitful to ask whether or to what degree Augustine's thinking changed on the importance of each conversion or their ordering to each other.[8] For instance, on the question of whether intellectual conversion is necessary in order for one to be relatively happy in this life, *On Order* would seem to answer in the affirmative, but the *Confessions* would seem to answer in the negative. And as to whether one needs to be morally converted before one can undergo an intellectual conversion, *Against the Academics* and *On Order* would seem to answer yes despite the fact that in the *Confessions* these conversions are narrated in the reverse order.[9]

THE DIALOGUE GENRE
The Platonic Template

Augustine chose the philosophical dialogue as the means of goading his readers to this triple conversion. To understand why, it is necessary to gain a better appreciation of this peculiar genre. The dialogue form as developed by Plato may be described as a way of effecting a sort of ceasefire in what Socrates calls "the old quarrel between philosophy and poetry."[10] Poetry, when conceived broadly to include all forms of narrative, holds considerable sway over the hearts of men and women by dint of its power to stir their emotions and imagination. Poetry thus becomes a major source of "values" for a people, functioning as the lens through which its followers filter, interpret, and evaluate their experiences. This reliance on the poets' authority and their fiction has the subtle effect of deterring men and women from independent and rational inquiry, the result being that more attention is paid to the poet's book than to the book of the world. Poetry therefore tends to be at odds with philosophy—that way of life which seeks a knowledge of the nature of things free of both opinion and authority. The concrete manifestation of this antagonism is a popular hatred of the philosopher (as we see in the trial of Socrates at Athens) and a philosophical censure of the poet (as we see in Socrates's criticisms of Homer). Further, because it generally appeals to the lowest and basest passions, poetry would seem to have a dubious effect on the moral development of its readers or hearers.

The Platonic dialogue, on the other hand, remains faithful to Socrates's way of life while successfully overcoming his reservations about poetry. The philosophical dialogue does not have the over-powering pathos of an epic or tragedy, a restraint that keeps readers' minds less lulled and more alert. Moreover, the dialectical quality of a dialogue, in which a single question often begets several contra-dictory answers, places on readers a certain onus to figure out the dialogue's true import, to sift through the various answers and scru-tinize them closely. Rather than be hypnotized by charm and beauty, readers are prompted by the dialogue to be perceptive and rational.[11]

This prompting may be said to consist of three dimensions. The first dimension of breadth or horizontality, of back-and-forth, requires readers to connect what they are reading now to what has gone before and to modify their impressions in light of what comes next. The second dimension of verticality, or up-and-down, requires readers to connect the narrative to the realities up to which they are pointing as well as to be cognizant of tensions or hints that are percolating below the surface. Finally, the third dimension of depth, from there-to-here, requires readers to discover or verify things for themselves, not in a relativistic or subjectivist way, but in light of the narrative clues and "cognitive norms of thought" (to borrow Kenyon's phrase) that are immanent in their own ability to know. Indeed, it is this third dimension—which in ocular vision gives depth perception—that can lead to self-knowledge.

The three-dimensionality of a philosophical dialogue is thus designed to bring readers to a state of knowing or discovery. But is it also designed to conceal? A philosophical dialogue can fall into anyone's hands, including the hands of someone for whom certain truths, at least at this stage in his or her life, would only do harm.[12] Further, since all political society (even that of an enlightened democracy) rests on dogmatic assumptions that must remain more or less publicly unquestioned for the sake of civic stability, philosophers must exercise considerable caution lest their philosophizing undermine the opinions necessary for a vibrant polity.

Consequently, it has been speculated that authors like Plato wrote in such a way that the more dangerous, destabilizing aspects of philosophy were carefully kept from the general readership and revealed to only a minority of readers through various clues in the text. A single dialogue could therefore have two different "messages": an "external" one for the philosophically challenged and an "internal" one for the philosophically inclined. In antiquity, these two different teachings came to be known as "exoteric" and "esoteric," respectively. Conceived thus, the philosophical dialogue may be compared to a tamper-proof aspirin bottle: its real content can be obtained only by those who are mature enough to figure out the directions, while the rest are kept from something that would only damage their health.[13]

The Augustinian Dialogue

Whatever conclusions one may wish to draw about a "secret teaching" in the writings of ancient philosophers, it cannot be denied that the Cassiciacum dialogues are self-consciously situated within a broad tradition of philosophical *poesis* that includes the possibility of esotericism. Augustine was keenly aware of the three-dimensional, protreptic value of the dialogue genre. In *On Order* 1.11.31 he mocks those who pay no attention to what in a dialogue "is being explained and accomplished" (the vertical dimension) as well as those who ignore the whence and "whither of the discussants' efforts" (the horizontal). Augustine also emphasizes readers' independent discovery of the truth vis-à-vis the texts (depth perception). As he tells Romanianus in *Against the Academics,* everything accomplished in the dialogues will remain a mere opinion in the mind of a reader rather than genuine knowledge until the reader enters "entirely into philosophy" and verifies the truth personally (2.3.8).

Moreover, as his interpretation of Cicero and the Academic skeptics attests, Augustine also knew of the esoteric possibilities of philosophical literature. He even appears to have appropriated some aspects of esoteric writing. Like Plato and Cicero, Augustine draws a line between the very rare kind of human being who can understand reality as it truly is and the vast majority who do not, and he likewise recognizes the danger in teaching the truth to those who are not ready for it. But there is one event separating Augustine and the philosophers that might explain how he differs from them: the Incarnation. God's humbling Himself and taking the form of a servant allows the carnal multitude for the first time to "return to their very selves and even gaze upon their homeland without the bickering of disputations." The divine Word becoming human flesh does not eliminate the fallen world's hatred of the light, and thus a careful reserve in expressing the truth is still necessary. But it does place a certain responsibility on the believer to bear witness to the truth and to avoid incurring any suspicion that the good news being preached is concocted. For Augustine, having an "exoteric" message that is meant to deceive nonphilosophical readers, even if well intentioned, is incompatible with the demands of the Gospel.[14]

Augustine's principled opposition to mendacity does not mean, however, that his dialogues are entirely veracious. In the *Soliloquies*, Augustine notes that not all falsehoods are lies: joke tellers, for instance, are not considered liars because their intention is not to deceive, and the same holds true for comic playwrights. Augustine himself admits that he can be ironic in these works. Overtly playful elements abound, such as the discussion in *On Order* about whether it is permissible to chant sacred music while answering the call of nature, but others are more veiled. A distant disciple of Augustine, St. Thomas More, was characterized as feigning seriousness so well when he was joking that his listeners had difficulty knowing when he spoke "in sport" and when "in good earnest." One wonders whether the same could not be said about Augustine at Cassiciacum. Key to any philosophical dialogue is its comic quality, a trait no doubt partially due to the philosopher's bemused indifference to the petty things, such as money or health or recognition, that most human beings regard with inordinate seriousness: a truly great soul, Cicero reminds his son, "holds as trivial the things that to the many seem to be outstanding and important." But more fundamentally, the dialogue's comic structure forces readers to get the joke, to discover on their own the knowledge being sought, and thus experience the delight of comprehension. Or put differently, with its beguiling three dimensions the dialogue is an ideal vehicle for exercising and provoking readers to the insights that induce or prepare for conversion. And this spiritual exercise includes mental curveballs that put us through our paces and render us sharper by befuddling us and prompting us to consult our own intelligence and the world that is. The Cassiciacum dialogues may not contain "noble lies," but they may contain noble untruths to test and challenge us.[15]

Reading a Cassiciacum Dialogue

At the very least, the dialogic character of the Cassiciacum corpus requires us to approach it as we would any other dramatic narrative. Never, for example, can we assume that the opinions of the interlocutors are those of Augustine the author, and neither can we even take for granted that the opinions of Augustine the character are those of Augustine the author. In deliberate imitation of daily life, what a character chooses to say is often contingent on who is present and who is not, on what personal motives are operative, and on what has just transpired. Consequently, abstracting from the dialogue's dramatic dimensions misleadingly reduces a subtle interplay of dynamics to a colorless series of propositions, thereby stripping the dialogue of a content that often lies in the penumbra of the text. As with any other narrative, a dialogue's characters, setting, plot, and time—not to mention the various incidentals mentioned throughout—are crucial.

Uncovering the many meanings of the dialogue therefore requires being fully and almost urgently attentive to the action of the work. As with a theatrical play, the Cassiciacum dialogues are to be experienced as if they were transpiring before our very eyes. Augustine follows the common ancient convention of putting narrative interjections such as "he says" in the present tense, but he amplifies this sense of presence with frequent exhortations to "pay attention" and "be here." Even more, Augustine says that we should put ourselves *into* the text. We will learn many things, Augustine tells Zenobius, if we engraft ourselves onto, and "co-fit" ourselves into, these works.[16]

It also helps to read the dialogues together. Augustine wrote the tetralogy in such a way that the teachings of one are clarified or even modified by those of another. We have already mentioned that the Cassiciacum dialogues function as a kind of spiritual exercise for readers, and exercise suffers when parts of a workout program are cut out randomly. Oddly, history has been fairly deaf to this obvious fact. Of the manuscript traditions bequeathed to us from the Middle Ages, not a single one includes all four dialogues together. *Against the Academics* and *On Order* were generally paired with each other while *On the Happy Life* was relegated elsewhere. Finally, the *Soliloquies* was either published alone or with later compositions of Augustine, but never with any of the other three dialogues. This dismemberment of the Cassiciacum corpus continued into the twentieth century with most editions of modern translations. From this pattern of publication we may tentatively conclude that for the bulk of their existence and despite their author's explicit intentions, the dialogues have not been read as a coherent unit. Consequently, one of the goals behind this present four-volume edition is to reunite what the accidents of history have put asunder.

Lastly, it is profitable to read the dialogues in order. Like several of Plato's and Cicero's dialogues, the Cassiciacum tetralogy is meant to be read in a particular sequence for the full effect. Intellectual, moral, and religious conversion begins with a rejection of skepticism, which deadens the desire for truth by preaching its unattainability (*Against the Academics*); progresses with an intensified desire to become happy and know God, who is the Truth (*On the Happy*

Life); turns on an understanding of God's order through the soul's coming to know itself (*On Order*); and is ratified with a more explicit affirmation of the soul's knowledge of itself and its participation in God (*Soliloquies*).[17]

AUGUSTINE'S SOURCES

Another constructive way to approach the Cassiciacum dialogues is with respect to the history out of which they emerged. Because of Augustine's numerous achievements over the course of his life, it is tempting to read the dialogues as primitive or even flawed anticipations of later works such as the *Confessions, On the Trinity,* and the *City of God.* Granted that Augustine's theology did indeed develop over time, this temptation must nevertheless be resisted, for the works at Cassiciacum are in their own right the culmination of a long and eventful intellectual journey. From his youth, Augustine had been schooled in the liberal arts. At the age of eighteen, he discovered philosophy and turned (briefly) to a study of the Bible; a year later, he read Aristotle's *Categories* and joined the Manichaeans; a year after that, he began teaching literature, rhetoric, and dialectic, first in his hometown of Thagaste and then in the thriving metropolis of Carthage. When he was about twenty-seven, his philosophical leanings inspired him to write his first book (now lost) called *On the Beautiful and the Fitting.* Approximately five years later, he became an Academic skeptic and then a Platonist; at about the same time, he was introduced to a circle of Christian intellectuals loosely centered around St. Ambrose. By the fall of A.D. 386, then, Augustine had spent years wrestling with the trivium and quadrivium, the dogmatic claims of the Manichaean sect, the disputations of various philosophical schools, and finally, his mother's faith. For the Augustine who penned them, the Cassiciacum dialogues are in a sense mature writings, the fruit of more than a decade of determined germination.

Cicero

Augustine's journey to Christianity involved confronting a diverse assortment of intellectual forces, almost all of which appear in the dialogues in some form or another. The most obvious is Marcus Tullius Cicero (106–43 B.C.), who, though often dismissed today as an intellectual dilettante, was held by Augustine to be a serious philosopher. Augustine's own passion for wisdom began with reading Cicero's *Hortensius* at the age of eighteen, and at Cassiciacum he continues to treat the *Hortensius* as foundational to the formation of the youths in his care. Further, with their cover letters, choice of setting, and use of long concluding speeches, the Cassiciacum dialogues bear an unmistakable resemblance to a Ciceronian, as opposed to a Platonic, dialogue. (Another indication is that Augustine, like Cicero and unlike Plato, casts himself as a prominent character with lines in his own dialogues.) Augustine himself admits the Ciceronian connection when in the *Confessions* he recounts a disagreement with his friend Alypius. As a sort of assistant editor, Alypius had wanted to omit the name of Jesus Christ from the dialogues so that they would be redolent of the lofty "cedars of the gymnasia," an allusion to the setting of several of Cicero's dialogues; but Augustine opted instead for what he called the "Church's wholesome herbs." The name of Christ remained, although it did not entirely eradicate the fragrance of cedar.[18]

Moreover, each of the first three Cassiciacum dialogues may be seen as a specific response to a work or cluster of works by Cicero. Augustine's *Against the Academics* obviously wrestles with Cicero's *Academica*, while *On the Happy Life* engages Cicero's *On the Ends of Good and Evil Things* and the *Tusculan Disputations*, both of which address the *summum bonum* and the art of "living happily." Similarly, *On Order* is a development of the themes in Cicero's *On the Nature of the Gods, On Divination,* and *On Fate,* which were intended to be read together. As with his use of the dialogue genre, Augustine's responses both build upon and move beyond their Ciceronian foundation. In *On Order,* for example, Augustine agrees with Cicero's critique of fate and superstition but replaces Cicero's insincere deference to Roman civil religion with a principled and unfeigned embrace of Christian teaching. And perhaps in a backhanded way it was Augustine's comfortable command of Ciceronian thought and composition that emboldened him to greater innovation with the *Soliloquies,* a dialogue that is unique in almost every way, from its neologic title to its sustained inner monologue and from its pioneering introspection to its thespian conceit. For as Augustine notes, it is after one masters something that one is eager to move on.[19]

The Platonists

But Augustine might never have been able to offer such a sustained engagement of Cicero or to overcome the philosophical skepticism of the school to which Cicero adhered were it not for the "Neoplatonists." This term is modern in origin, but it aptly signals a difference between the Platonists of the third and fourth centuries after Christ and Plato himself (427–347 B.C.). Whereas Plato, for instance, wrote only dialogues that enmeshed his metaphysical discussions in a political context, the Neoplatonists wrote abstract treatises or commentaries that were highly technical and often apolitical in nature. But whatever their differences with Plato, the one Platonic insight that the Neoplatonists affirmed and expanded is the one that made all the difference to Augustine: the insight into intelligible reality wrought by intellectual conversion. After that insight, nothing would ever be the same: "When behold! Some fulsome books, as Celsinus puts it, as soon as they breathed forth upon us good Arabian [fragrances] and as soon as they dribbled just a few drops of their most precious ointment onto the tiny flicker, they enkindled an incredible, Romanianus, an incredible (and beyond what perhaps even you believe about me—what more can I say?—beyond what I as well believe about myself!), an *incredible* conflagration." The incredible conflagration of which Augustine speaks is the intellectual conversion mentioned above, which yields a rare kind of knowledge of one's own understanding or knowing as incorporeal or immaterial. This self-knowledge plays a role in all four dialogues, but it is especially prominent in *On Order* and the *Soliloquies*. And it also had a profound albeit implicit impact on Augustine's understanding of the three divine persons in the doctrine of the Trinity.[20]

It should be noted that scholars are not entirely certain which Neoplatonists influenced Augustine the most or, for that matter, how much of Plato Augustine ever read. Curiously, unlike his use of Cicero and the poets (see below), Augustine never directly quotes his Platonic sources. His writings betray a deep familiarity with several of the tractates of Plotinus (A.D. 204/205–270), but the influence of Porphyry (A.D. 232/234–305) and possibly others cannot be overlooked either. Regardless, Augustine's debt to Plato or the Neoplatonists, no matter how great, does not imply that his own thought is reducible to them. Perhaps the best analogy for the relationship of St. Augustine to his classical sources is that of a skilled musician riffing off different melodic phrases in a way that is not beholden to their composers' intentions.[21]

The Poets

Augustine's sources were not limited to the philosophical. The assortment of Roman scholars and historians from which Augustine draws includes Aulus Gellius, Apuleius, Celsus, Pliny, Quintilian, Sallust, Seneca, Tacitus, Varro, and Vitruvius. Moreover, the old quarrel between philosophy and poetry reemerges at Cassiciacum, with Augustine mustering Latin authors on both sides of the battle. A tragic love story by Ovid (43 B.C.–A.D. 17) occasions a dispute between Augustine and Licentius, and lines from the plays of Terence (195/185–159 B.C.) frequently reinforce the dialogues' comic character. The writings of Horace, Plautus, and even Lucretius are alluded to. Motifs from classical mythology are not uncommon either: Hector, Andromache, Hercules, Achilles, Medusa, Mount Helicon and the Muses, Scylla and Charybdis, Daedalus, and especially Proteus are all mentioned.

But the most important poet at Cassiciacum is Vergil (70–19 B.C.), whom the retreatants read daily and who appears to be viewed by Augustine as a poet with philosophical promise, either someone who in his own way had built a bridge between philosophy and poetry or whose verses could be used for that purpose — or perhaps, it was simply the case that the privileged status that Vergil's poems enjoyed in contemporary Roman life made them virtually irresistible. Whatever the reason, of all the poets at his disposal, Augustine appears most eager to "repurpose" Vergil by treating his work as an opportunity for ruminating on Christian truth.[22]

Throughout the dialogues and regardless of the poet in question, Augustine evinces a keen awareness of the power of poetry on its readers' emotions and judgment and its claims on their allegiance. Yet he refrains from treating poetry as an enemy; instead, he employs a variety of techniques to channel or "convert" the power and beauty of the poets in a direction more open to philosophy and the Christian faith. The dialogues themselves— which, as we have already noted, are innovative not only philosophically and theologically but literarily as well—are the most impressive result of this endeavor. Augustine's own dialogic *poesis* is his ultimate and most eloquent answer at Cassiciacum to the ancient quarrel between philosophy and poetry.

Lastly, Augustine's brocading the dialogues with Greco-Roman poetic fancies serves the additional purpose of establishing this Christian author as well educated and familiar with the literary canon that was the staple of Roman high society. Although Augustine later came to regret many of his nods to classical literature, his generous use of ancient poetry and his well-crafted prosody were part of a common patristic strategy to use the literary arts of Christianity's detractors against them.[23]

The Christians

The disagreement of Augustine and Alypius over the inclusion of Christ's name might give the impression that the Christian dimension of the dialogues can be excised with only a few cosmetic changes and is therefore superficial at best. Lending support to this conclusion are the cover letters to *Against the Academics* and *On Order,* which exhort their recipients to "philosophize" or "return to themselves" but make no mention of the Christian God.

Such a view, however, would be misleading. Although they are not explicitly catechetical or apologetic, and although they frequently appeal to reason without a direct connection to divine revelation, the Cassiciacum dialogues have a pervasively Christian content. Not only is the group portrayed as praying daily and holding discussions on God and Jesus Christ, but Augustine consistently aligns the dynamic of human knowing with the processions of the divine persons of the Trinity as understood by orthodox Christianity.[24] Augustine may call *On the Happy Life* more religious than the others (1.5), but all of the dialogues involve an interplay between, and an integration of, faith and reason.

It should also be noted that even though he was operating under the constraints of the discipline of the secret, Augustine already had at Cassiciacum a significant exposure to Christian thought. He knew the four canonical Gospels (or at least parts of them), several Psalms (which he prayed daily), and several sections of the Epistles of St. Paul. As he recounts in the *Confessions*, he was deeply influenced by the sermons of St. Ambrose (337/340–397) as well as by Marius Victorinus, the story of whose conversion to Christianity profoundly affected Augustine. In fact, it was Victorinus's translations of several Neoplatonic books that prompted Augustine's intellectual conversion around 385 or 386, and there is evidence in the Cassiciacum tetralogy that Augustine was also familiar with Victorinus's Christian writings on the Trinity. Finally, Augustine and Monica socialized with Christian intellectuals such as Manlius Theodorus, to whom he dedicates *On the Happy Life*.[25]

As far as Christian or patristic literature goes, the Cassiciacum dialogues are fairly novel, especially with respect to diction. Mary Bogan counts more than thirty neologisms in the four works, a higher concentration than is found in Augustine's later writings. Augustine, for instance, coined the word "soliloquy" to designate his fourth dialogue, which is itself an unprecedented melding of a philosophical dialogue and a stage play: he also appears to be the originator of the theological expression "beatific vision." Even in the realm of the mundane, Augustine left his mark while at Cassiciacum: from what we can tell, he is the first author to describe what is known today as a cuckoo clock. Coupled with a relative dearth of ecclesiastical terminology, with which he would become familiar only after his baptism and ordination to the priesthood, Augustine's semantic resourcefulness attests to an eagerness to communicate something of great importance and a slight uncertainty with how best to go about it. Even as a catechumen, Augustine could not wait to proclaim the Gospel from the Areopagus to the Seven Hills of Rome.[26]

On the Happy Life

INTRODUCTION

"Everyone wants to live happily, my brother Gallio, but they are in the dark when it comes to seeing what it is that makes a life happy." The opening words of *On the Happy Life* by the Stoic philosopher Seneca the Younger (ca. 1 B.C.–A.D. 65) express both the goal and the frustration that belongs uniquely to the human race. On one hand and in contradistinction to the rest of the animal kingdom, human beings yearn to be happy—not simply free of discomfort like a cow at pasture, but honestly and fulsomely happy. This yearning is true without exception: even the masochist and the suicide are, in a perverse or tragic way, seeking happiness. On the other hand, most men and women fall short of this universal goal and die unhappy, in large part because they have not properly identified the nature of happiness and have tried in vain a number of substitutes. Seneca's proposed solution to this general problem is to disregard the opinions of the mass of humanity, who (in Thoreau's words) lead lives of quiet desperation, and to discover objectively that for which we really should be aiming. Moreover, given the brevity of life and the uncertainty of individual judgment, this discovery should be sought with the help of a competent and wise guide.

On the Happy Life

LITERATURE ON HAPPINESS

Seneca's interest in the subject of happiness and his mode of inquiry are two of several precedents that Augustine had in mind when he wrote his dialogue *On the Happy Life*, the title of which is distinguishable from Seneca's only by word order (Seneca wrote *De vita beata*, Augustine *De beata vita*). Augustine knew that he was not breaking any new ground simply by writing on how to be happy. A keen concern for authentic human happiness may be said to lie at the heart of all ancient philosophy from Socrates on. It was Socrates, Cicero noted, who first "called down philosophy from the heavens" and compelled it to inquire into the various human efforts to be happy;[1] and it is in Plato's dialogues that we see these efforts vetted and scrutinized by Socrates's famous method of examination. Aristotle's *Nicomachean Ethics* is widely regarded as antiquity's most thorough examination of happiness, but Aristotle tells us that he also wrote much on the good life in his dialogues (now lost) and that these are summarized in sections of his *Politics*.[2] Four of Cicero's dialogues concern happiness—his lost *Hortensius*, *On the Ends of Good and Evil Things* (*De finibus bonorum et malorum*), *On Duties* (*De officiis*) and, especially, the *Tusculan Disputations*. Centuries later Plotinus composed, through the mediation of his disciple Porphyry, a tractate on happiness that would have a significant influence on Augustine's developing thought.[3] Stoics, Epicureans, and Cynics expatiated on the subject, and even the skeptics, Pyrrhonian and Academic alike, joined in. Indeed, happiness was the main motivation behind the ancient skeptic's extensive intellectual doubts: Descartes may have unleashed his radical skepticism in order to gain the power of certainty and, eventually, a technological domination over nature, but premodern skepticism strove to avoid bad judgments at all cost because of the personal misery that comes from being in error.

Finally, early Christian authors gladly engaged this tradition on the grounds that the faith bequeathed to them by the apostles was the key to the happiness discussed by the philosophers. Book seven of the *Divine Institutes* by the "Christian Cicero" Lactantius is titled "On the Happy Life" (*De beata vita*), and St. Ambrose of Milan wrote his homiletic *On Jacob and the Happy Life* around the same time, it is believed, that Augustine was writing this dialogue.

EUDAIMONISM

One of the things that Church Fathers like Ambrose could agree on with their philosophical interlocutors was an appreciation of reason and virtue, for "a mind intent on reason excels in the virtues and restrains the passions."[4] Contrary to our strong visceral tendencies to identify happiness as a good feeling or emotion, the sages of both Athens and Jerusalem taught that happiness was an activity determined by one's whole character. Aristotle lists "living well" or "doing well" as synonymous with *eudaimonia*, the Greek word for happiness; and what constitutes doing something well is doing something with *arēte*, that is, with excellence or virtue.[5] A long life of moral and intellectual excellence, then, is a life of happiness; and the discipline of ethics is nothing else but the science on how to be happy.

This position, which is known today as eudaimonism, is alien to much of our contemporary sensibilities, for we are now less prone to think of our morals in relation to our happiness. Current public debates on ethics are usually governed by the overarching if unspoken question of what we are morally obligated to do even though we do not want to do it, while deliberations about happiness are relegated to the relativism of private choice or personal autonomy and the manipulation of advertisers promising nirvana

with each new product. Even Christians can become too concerned
with getting themselves into heaven rather than getting heaven
into them. Nor is this truncated approach limited to popular circles.
Modern ethicists tend to focus on the rightness or wrongness of
actions per se, whereas ancient moralists also looked at an action
vis-à-vis the effect that it was having on the soul or character of the
agent, that is, on how it was affecting his or her prospects at real
happiness.[6]

But the classical focus on *eudaimonia* does not mean that
there was universal agreement on its nature. In identifying happiness with pleasure (especially of the bodily variety), the Epicureans
dissented from the philosophical tradition inaugurated by Plato
and Aristotle in which happiness involved experiencing the right
pleasures at the right time in the right way and in which bodily
pleasure was ranked below the mind's delight in discovering truth.
And even among the non-Epicureans there were other disagree-
ments. Granted that virtue is essential for happiness, is it the highest
good or the only good? If it is the former, then other goods, such as
a modicum of wealth or health, are necessary to living happily;
such was the position of the Peripatetics, the disciples of Aristotle.
If it is the latter, then all one needs to be happy is virtue, and one
can therefore be happy in abject poverty, in the grips of a fatal
disease, and while being tortured on the rack; such was the view
famously taught by the Stoics. And exactly how high do we set the
bar for a person to be considered authentically happy? Aristotle,
who speaks of happiness as an excellent activity of the soul and not
a mere mood or feeling, nevertheless reminds his readers that the
happiness in question is proportionate to human nature; it is not
the happiness of the gods, nor is it even the state of being blessed
by the gods.[7] On the other hand, Cicero, evincing here a Platonic
predilection for the unqualified noun, holds that it is foolhardy to

think of happiness in degrees: to be truly happy is to be supremely happy or not happy at all.[8]

Further, what is the role of the intellectual virtues, of perfected reason, in conferring happiness? Can a person be happy without being wise? Can he or she be wise and happy without being morally virtuous? And is reason, even when perfected, up to the task of governing all of the soul's sometimes herculean passions and appetites in such a way that one can become habitually good or virtuous? A well-known passage from John Henry Newman is worth remembering in this context: "Quarry the granite rock with razors, or moor the vessel with a thread of silk; then may you hope with such keen and delicate instruments as human knowledge and human reason to contend against those giants, the passion and the pride of man."[9]

Lastly and perhaps most importantly, is happiness even attainable? If not in this life, what about the next? Interestingly, the proposed answers to this question often cut across philosophical and religious lines. Aristotle, even with his relatively scaled-back standard of happiness (at least in comparison to the Stoics), was probably less sanguine than he initially appears. Acquiring virtue requires imitating someone virtuous, and so if no one is virtuous—and who among us truly is?—no one else, according to Aristotle's logic, can become virtuous.[10] St. Ambrose, on the other hand, takes the Stoic teaching that the perfected man is happy in this life and applies it to the holy figures of the Old Testament. Ambrose resolves the tension between Athens and Jerusalem by preaching that the perfection only talked about by the philosophers is found concretely, thanks to God, in the lives of the patriarch Jacob and others—so much so, in fact, that just as the Stoic wise man could be happy on the rack, so too was the prophet Isaiah happy while being sawed in half, Jeremiah while being drowned, and the seven brothers Maccabee and their mother while undergoing unspeakable torments.[11] (Augustine, as we shall see, may in some respects be closer to Aristotle than to Ambrose on this question.)

THE TUSCULAN PRECEDENT

In writing *On the Happy Life*, Augustine was self-consciously engrafting himself onto this long line of discussion, but he was especially cognizant of Cicero's *Tusculan Disputations*. Cicero was keen in that dialogue to show that happiness is a matter not of luck but of character and that subsequently people with strong moral fiber and good judgment can remain happy no matter what misfortunes befall them. Part of Cicero's goal in making this argument is to persuade his somewhat leery Roman audience of the necessity of the philosophical life: since only the wise are virtuous, Cicero is telling his compatriots, and since philosophy is the love of wisdom, philosophy is essential for the inculcation of virtue and happiness in Roman civic society.[12] By the same token, we can say that Cicero is trying to promote a philosophical understanding of things by discrediting an antiphilosophical and tragic worldview that construes the universe as dark and unintelligible and that subsequently views human flourishing as a product of capricious Fates—hence Cicero's persistent opposition in book five of the *Tusculan Disputations* to any position that would give chance or fortune a foothold in the determination of happiness. If we concede a role to the goddess Fortuna, Cicero fears, the bulk of citizens will spend all their time bribing, begging, and cajoling her rather than acquiring the virtues that conduce to a happy life.[13] It also explains some of Cicero's more extreme statements, such as that nothing is good except what is totally within one's own power.[14] If I do not have complete control over something, then Fortuna has her mercurial hand on it, and if Fortuna has her hand on it, I can in no way rely on it for my happiness.

But there are problems with the Tusculan project, problems of which Cicero himself is not unaware. To render happiness immune from the vicissitudes of chance, Cicero in the *Tusculan Disputations* rejects the Peripatetic teaching on external goods as a component of happiness (since such goods, as we have just seen, are subject to misfortune) and embraces the hard line of the Stoics in which the only good is virtue and the only one who can be virtuous and happy is the wise man.[15] Philosophy, Cicero goes on to claim, promises that it can make men and women wise, virtuous, and happy, yet he evades the question of whether philosophy ever makes good on its promise—even though he is the one who raised it.[16] Despite Cicero's robust portrayal of happiness, the *Tusculan Disputations* amounts to saying that *if* human happiness exists, it would have such-and-such a profile.

THE AUGUSTINIAN BANQUET

Augustine's debt to the *Tusculan Disputations* is clear. The opening images of *On the Happy Life*—fleeing to the bosom of philosophy and sailing to its haven after being tossed by a great storm—are taken directly from this dialogue.[17] The three consecutive days of discussion in *On the Happy Life* echo the five consecutive days of disputation at Tusculum, and so does much of the content. Augustine's treatment of the soul's "food" as the knowledge and understanding of things recapitulates much of the third book of the *Tusculan Disputations* and yields a similar consideration of frugality.[18] Indeed, a good many of the ingredients in Augustine's spiritual banquet (the central metaphor in *On the Happy Life*) have been borrowed from the Tusculum pantry, such as that the wise man is always happy, his soul is perfect, his bodily wants or the caprices of chance do not undermine his peace of mind, and he is strong and unafraid of death or pain.[19]

But as every chef knows, identical ingredients can be prepared in strikingly different ways. The differences between these dialogues are obvious from the start: whereas Cicero speaks only of the port of philosophy, Augustine espies a dry land beyond it where one encounters Christian intellectuals such as Theodorus, to whom he has dedicated the dialogue, and possibly St. Ambrose, whose intelligent and refined sermons had inspired Augustine to reevaluate his dismissal of Christian dogma as uncouth nonsense.[20] Like Cicero, Augustine cherishes philosophy for granting the soul safe harbor from the tempests of misfortune, but unlike him he also lauds philosophy as the dock for an even grander destination: the terra firma of divine revelation and grace. The introduction to *On the Happy Life* begins by praising philosophy but ends with an allusion to the dialogue's religious content.[21]

The finished product is a response to the studied ambivalence of the *Tusculan Disputations*. Augustine answers Cicero's question about whether philosophy can fulfill its promise of happiness with a quiet but resolute "no." To borrow an image from the *Confessions*, philosophers can point to the destination of happiness, but they cannot arrive there themselves, for between them and their destination lies an impenetrable jungle haunted by the demonic.[22] Even at Cassiciacum, Augustine would find himself in agreement with Samuel Taylor Coleridge, who wrote: "By undeceiving, enlarging, and informing the intellect, Philosophy sought to purify and elevate the moral character. . . . Across the night of Paganism, Philosophy flitted on, like the lantern-fly of the Tropics, a light to itself, and an ornament, but, alas, no more than an ornament, of the surrounding darkness."[23]

But Augustine has good news: although philosophy, beautiful yet impotent, cannot keep its promise, Christianity can. Augustine and his friends at Cassiciacum agree with much of Cicero's profile of the happy life but conclude that it can be fully realized only in the knowledge and love of the God of Abraham, Isaac, and Jacob. Paradoxically, the wise man maintains and even expands his freedom and his immunity from fortune by replacing his impossible goal of total self-sufficiency with a dependence on the liberating grace of God.

Moreover, the human soul's deepest yearnings and aspirations can be satisfied only by a perfect "possession" of the Blessed Trinity. (*On the Happy Life* is essentially an elaborate gloss on the most famous line in the *Confessions*, that our hearts are restless until they rest in God.) It is not surprising that a catechumen filled with zeal for his newfound faith would make such an argument; what perhaps is surprising is the degree to which that catechumen employs the aid of the philosophers to formulate it. *On the Happy Life* evinces a remarkable deference to the capacity of reason to identify problems and outline solutions. On one hand, Augustine uses philosophical reasoning on its own terms, content to allow its ultimate implications to unfold and fall where they may. On the other hand, he is equally determined to view the subject of happiness in light of the Gospel—not because he is an opponent of humanism, but because he recognizes that an exclusive humanism, one that precludes religious questions from even being asked, is an inhuman humanism. For Augustine, introducing the Trinity into the human science of happiness is not only valid but inevitable.

More specifically, underlying Augustine's thesis are both Ciceronian and Neoplatonic tenets. From Cicero comes the idea that the happy soul possesses frugality or moderation; from Plotinus comes the idea that wisdom, as the highest form of knowledge, is the grasp of ultimate Being or ultimate Intelligibility. The soul, we come to learn, has a natural orientation toward this ultimate X or God, an orientation that is made obvious from its potentially unrestricted desire to know everything. But this desire cannot be fulfilled unaided: even the totality of scientific progress from now until the end of time cannot answer all of the human intellect's driving questions about the why, whence, and whither of things; and even if it could, it would not necessarily mean that I myself, with all my personal demons and limited perspective and finite lifespan, could ever reach such a zenith. In contrast to Plotinus's teachings, in order for humanity to become truly happy, it must not only ascend up to the divine, but the divine must descend down to it: Wisdom must become incarnate to meet us where we are and lift us up.

All of which is present most clearly in the discussion on the third and final day, when Augustine fleshes out Cicero's concepts of frugality and worthlessness in light of Plotinus's ideas on being and nonbeing at the same time that he modifies Plotinus's ideas in light of the Christian doctrine of the Trinity.[24] In *On the Happy Life* we therefore witness a double transformation: a metaphysical transformation of Cicero's moral philosophy with the help of Plotinus, and a theological transformation of Plotinus's metaphysics with the help of the new covenant.

THE PLACE OF *ON THE HAPPY LIFE*

On the Happy Life is the sequel to *Against the Academics* and is meant to be read that way, even though chronologically it takes place in between book one and book two of *Against the Academics* (see the Time Line). In *Against the Academics*, readers discover that the human mind can indeed assent to the truth but that no individual, not even a philosopher, can be happy by merely searching for the truth. *On the Happy Life* presupposes and builds upon both conclusions. The "possession" of truth is essential for happiness, and that possession is made possible by God; for God, who is Truth, allows Himself to be "possessed" by those whom He has given the grace to know and love Him. Implicit in Augustine's treatment—and this he shares with philosophers like Cicero and Plotinus—is the conviction that happiness is a permanent state in which human nature is completed or perfected. This perfection especially involves satisfying the source of the mind's impressive dynamism, what can be called its most sublime lacuna—its unrestricted aching to know all, a desire that is completed only by human intelligence uniting with or latching onto total intelligibility. But it also involves a satisfaction of the soul's other desires, provided they are in conformity with the good (if they are not, they need to be eliminated rather than satisfied, since wicked or disordered desires are ultimately self-destructive and the bearers of misery). It might be objected that this standard is outrageously high, but that does not render it false. Augustine is less interested in our subjective preferences regarding happiness than in its objective requirements.

HAPPINESS NOW?

Given this high standard, it might also be wondered whether happiness ever can be attained in this life. As a priest and bishop years later, Augustine is clear: happiness not only eludes us this side of the grave, but there is a way in which not even the souls in heaven are perfectly happy until the Last Judgment and the resurrection of the body; until then, they wait in "patient longing" for reunion with their glorified flesh.[25] Augustine's position at Cassiciacum, however, is more ambiguous. Near the end of his life, Augustine chided himself for having written in the *Soliloquies* that any soul which understands God is happy now,[26] but even so, the statement in question occurs in a passage that lists a perfect love of God and an attainment of the beatific vision (*beatissima visio*) as constitutive of such an understanding—hardly easy feats for sinful mortals still dwelling in and warring against the flesh.

The safest conclusion we can make is that Augustine at Cassiciacum does not definitively state when happiness is attainable, nor does he have to in order to argue his case successfully. The mere transfer of happiness to the love and knowledge of a providential God delivers Augustine from the philosophical quagmire concerning the necessity and role of external goods, leapfrogging over both the unrealistic Stoic deprecation of external goods on one hand and the Theophrastan slide to the tyranny of fortune on the other.[27] For Augustine, the fact *that* happiness is attainable by the grace of God is of far greater importance than the question of *when* it is attained. Whereas Cicero must treat philosophy as a medicine of the soul that can be administered only by oneself in this life,[28] Augustine can portray knowledge as the food of the soul served by God in small portions now and in perfect portions later.[29]

None of this is to suggest, however, that Augustine is a pessimist who sees this life as nothing more than a vale of tears. The tone of the work alone should disabuse us of any such suspicions. Cicero wrote the *Tusculan Disputations* with a heart of sorrow as he coped with his daughter Tullia's death, and Seneca's *On the Happy Life*, written partially in response to accusations of hypocrisy for both owning wealth and preaching its irrelevance, is at times testy and defensive. Augustine's *On the Happy Life*, by contrast, is filled with mirth and joy. The group laughs and smiles frequently,[30] and the occasion, Augustine's thirty-second birthday, is one of celebration.

On the Happy Life is even distinctive within the Cassiciacum corpus, for it is the only dialogue in which no one weeps: *Against the Academics* and *On Order* mix laughter with tears,[31] while the *Soliloquies* contains tears but no laughter.[32] Even if no perfect happiness exists short of the last day, the Christian hope in that perfection gives gladness to the heart here and now.

THE BLISS OF HAPPINESS

On the Happy Life challenges us to question some of our most cherished assumptions about happiness, but to do that we must begin by acknowledging a linguistic handicap. No English word adequately denotes what Augustine, or his philosophical predecessors for that matter, mean by happiness. We have already noted that there is currently a strong tendency to think of happiness as synonymous with positive and ephemeral feelings; and, of course, we are inclined to think of happiness in terms of degrees and to employ comparative adjectives such as "happier." Further, the word "happiness" is derived from "hap," meaning fortune or chance, thus implying (over the protestations of Cicero) that happiness resides with the person who is lucky rather than morally good.

The word that Augustine uses for "happy" is *beatus*, which can also be translated, especially in the Christian tradition, as "blessed." *Beatus* is the word that Latin philosophers like Cicero and Seneca typically employed, although Seneca also made occasional use of the other Latin term for "happy," *felix*. Etymologically, *felix* may have been the better choice for the philosophical Greek notion of *eudaimonia*, for it originally referred to fertility or abundance and hence, one could argue, completion or perfection. Practically speaking, however, *felix* was overwhelmingly linked to favorable fortune: the Romans had even dedicated a temple to Felicitas, a good luck goddess.[33] Perhaps because of this pagan association, early Christian authors assiduously avoided using *felix* and preferred instead *beatus*. In the Vulgate translation of the Bible, *beatus* occurs 112 times and *felix* only 5.

Probably the best English equivalents of *beatus* are "beatific" and, even better, "blissful." "Bliss" suggests the perfect and perpetual happiness that the saints in heaven are enjoying (or will after the Parousia), and before the days of standardized spelling it was conflated with "bless." Nonetheless, for ease on the modern ear and in acquiescence to entrenched usage, in the following translation I use "happy" for *beatus* or, when necessary, "blessed." When, for instance, Augustine speaks of a *beata terra* beyond the port of wisdom,[34] I render it as "blessed land," since "happy land" sounds too much like the children's play area at a fast-food restaurant.

Yet perhaps it is well that we retain the language of happiness. When Augustine announces to his interlocutors that "we all want to be happy," he is barely able to get the words out before they voice their hearty agreement.[35] It is difficult to imagine anything but the mundane word "happy" eliciting so spontaneous a response, and it is precisely such a gut reaction that is needed to begin the important quest for *eudaimonia*. There must be a personal investment in the search for happiness, one that should be free of bias, to be sure, but not of a sense of existential exigency. That exigency is helpful when assessing Augustine's arguments, which require a special kind of personal corroboration. The claim that the mind's deepest yearnings and aspirations are happily satisfied by a perfect possession of God can be affirmed or denied only by adverting to the boundless nature of the reader's own intellectual hunger, or *eros*, responsible for all of his or her curiosity, learning, and mental frustration. In Augustine's hands, the age-old question of happiness becomes an intriguing invitation to a unique form of self-knowledge. Let the banquet begin.

On the Happy Life

1. If a course charted by reason and if the will itself could bring someone to the port of philosophy[1] (the port from which one is already advancing onto the region and solid ground of the happy life),[2] then I do not know whether or not I am rash in saying, O Theodorus, you most refined and great man, that men are going to reach it in very small numbers—although actually, as we see nowadays, the men who reach it *are* few and far between.[3] For when either God or nature or necessity[4] or our will or some combination of these or all of them together (for the matter is very obscure, although it is being undertaken now so that you may nevertheless shed light on it) randomly tosses us into this world to and fro, so to speak, as if we were on a stormy sea, how few would ever come to know in what direction they should be striving or by what way they should be returning unless at one time or other, against their will and in spite of their resistance, some storm— which to the foolish seems adverse—should thrust the ignorant and the erroneous onto that land so devoutly to be wished?[5]

2. Therefore, it seems to me that there are three classes of seafaring men, as it were, whom philosophy is able to receive.[6] The first is the class of those who, when they reach an age fully possessed of reason, with a little sweep and stroke of the oars,[7] speed away from a location nearby and take refuge in the tranquility [of this port]. From here they raise a shining bright standard[8] of some work of theirs for as many of their other compatriots as they can,[9] so that in being admonished their compatriots may try to reach them.[10]

The second class, however, is of those who, unlike the seafarers mentioned above, are deceived by the utterly beguiling appearance of the sea. They have chosen to go out into its midst, and they dare to wander far from their homeland, often becoming forgetful of it.[11] If a wind that they reckon to be favorable somehow follows them from astern (in an exceedingly obscure manner), these men push off into the depths of misery elated and rejoicing, since all around a most deceitful calm of pleasures and honors is enticing them![12] Surely, what else should one wish for such men other than for some misfortune in the very things that are pulling them out to sea so cheerful? And if this does not suffice, what else should one wish for other than for a thoroughly raging tempest, a headwind that would lead them—even as they weep and mourn—to sure and solid joys? That said, since most men of this kind have not yet strayed out too far, they are led back by troubles that are not quite so serious. When tearful tragedies in their fortunes or anxiety-ridden difficulties in their hollow business affairs drive them to the books of learned and very wise men as if they had nothing else to do, they somehow wake up in the very port from which no promises of that sea, with its excessively fake smile, can keep them away.

But in between these two classes is a third. These men are either on the very threshold of youth or have already been tossed about a great deal and for a long time,[13] and yet they look back on certain standards and, even in the midst of the very waves, remember their most sweet homeland. And either they return to it by a direct course with no deception and without delay, or—quite often getting lost among the clouds or gazing at the sinking stars or, captivated by various allurements, letting opportunities for smooth sailing pass them by—they drift for too long, and not infrequently they are even in danger. Here again some calamity in the flux of fortunes often drives them, like a tempest averse to their endeavors, onto that devoutly wished for life of rest.

3. But for all of these men who are brought to the region of the happy life no matter how, there stands a vast mountain before the port that also causes great difficulties to those who would enter, a mountain that should be feared most intensely and avoided most carefully.[14] For it shines so brightly and is draped in so deceitful a light that not only does it present itself to those who have arrived and not yet entered as a place in which to live, and not only does it promise that it will satisfy their desires for the blessed land, but it even summons to itself a good many men from the port itself. And sometimes, it detains those delighted by the very height, from which they take pleasure in looking down upon everyone else.[15] Nevertheless, these men often admonish newcomers not to be deceived by the hidden rocks below or to think that they can climb up to them easily;[16] and, because of the proximity [of these proud men] to the land, they very kindly teach by which route it may be entered without danger. Thus, when they begrudge others [a share of their] utterly vain glory, they show them the place of security.

For with respect to those who are approaching philosophy or those who have already entered into it, what other mountain does reason want them to understand is to be feared if not the proud zeal for utterly empty glory? Such zeal has nothing full and solid within, so that it sinks and swallows up the puffed-up people who walk upon its cracking and brittle ground, and it snatches away from those who are thrown back into the darkness the bright home that they had almost now seen.[17]

4. Since this is the way things are, learn, my dear Theodorus—for I look to you alone for that which I desire, and I always admire you as a most accurate man—learn, I say, which of these three classes of men has sent me to you, and in what place it seems to me that I am, and what kind of help I confidently anticipate from you.

At the age of eighteen, after I had received in the school of rhetoric the famous book of Cicero called *The Hortensius*, I was set on fire with such a love of philosophy that I considered rushing to it at once.[18] But there was no lack of clouds to confound my course,[19] and for a long time, I confess, I looked up to the stars sinking into the ocean[20] and was led astray by them; for a certain childish superstition was also frightening me from inquiry itself. And when I was able to hold my head up higher,[21] I dispelled the gloom and persuaded myself to yield to those who actually taught rather than gave orders.[22] I had fallen in with men for whom this light of ours, which is perceived by the eyes, is seen as one of the divine realities that should be supremely worshiped.[23] I did not agree, but I reckoned that they were hiding something great in these wrappings and that they would open it up for me sometime.[24] But as soon as I struck them down and escaped them[25]—and especially after crossing that sea of ours—for a long time the Academics[26] held the helm of my ship as it resisted every gale in the midst of the waves.[27]

And then I came upon these lands. Here I learned of a North Star to which I could entrust myself.[28] For I have noticed often in the discourses of our priest[29] and sometimes in yours that when one is thinking about God, one should in no way think about the body[30]—nor when thinking about the soul*,[31] since it is the one thing that is close to God.[32]

But I must admit that I was detained by the allure of marriage and honor,[33] the result being that I did not dash off quickly to the bosom of philosophy. [My plan was] that only after I had attained these things would I then—as is permitted to a few of the most fortunate—set full sail and bend all oars toward the bay of philosophy and rest there.[34] But after I read a tiny number of the books of Plotinus,[35] for whom, I have learned, you have great enthusiasm, I compared them, insofar as I could, to the authority of those who have handed down the divine mysteries.[36] And I became so inflamed that I would have broken all these anchors were it not for the fact that the opinion of some men was troubling me.[37] What else, therefore, remained than that a tempest, which is *reputed* to be adverse, should come to my aid as I was dallying among the remaining trifles? And so a chest pain[38] seized me with such force that, being unable to bear the burden of my profession (by which I was possibly setting sail for the Sirens),[39] I jettisoned everything and steered my ship, battered and worn out, if you will, to the tranquility for which I longed.[40]

5. And so you see the philosophy that I would sail around in as if I were in a port. But this port is also wide open; and although its vastness is now less dangerous, it still does not fully keep out error. For I am utterly ignorant as to what part of the land (which alone is really happy) I should draw myself near to and touch ground on. For what solid ground have I held onto, I for whom the question about the soul* still pitches and lists?[41] Consequently, I implore you by your virtue, by your humane kindness, by the bond of our souls* and their interplay with each other, that you stretch forth your right hand to me—that is, that you love me and trust in turn that you are loved and held dear by me. If I am granted this request,

I shall come near with little effort and with great ease to that blessed land to which, I presume, you already cling.

In order for you to know what I am doing and how I am gathering my loved ones into this port of ours, and so that from this you may more fully understand my mind (for I find that there are no other signs by which I may disclose myself), I have reckoned that one of my disputations, which seems to me to have turned out to be more religious and more worthy of your renown, should be addressed to you and dedicated in your name. And indeed this is most fitting: for we have been inquiring among ourselves into the happy life, and I see nothing else that is more deservedly called a "gift of God."[42] I am not frightened by your eloquence, for I cannot be afraid of whatever I love, even if I do not attain it; and certainly, I am much less afraid of the loftiness of your [good] fortune. Indeed, however great your fortune is, it takes second place in your eyes; for truly, those who are dominated by fortune are those whom fortune puts in second place.[43]

But turn your attention, I beseech, to what I shall now say:

6. The Ides of November was my birthday.[44] After a lunch light enough to keep all of our wits about us,[45] I called all of us who had been living together not only on this day but every day to be seated at the baths, for it had occurred to me that this was a secluded place well suited for the season.[46] There were—for I am not afraid to make them known to your exceptional kindness, albeit in name alone—first of all, our mother, by whose merit, I believe, I am all that I am;[47] Navigius, my brother; Trygetius and Licentius, fellow townsmen and students of mine; and my cousins Lartidianus and Rusticus, who have not endured even a single grammar school teacher but whom I did not want to be absent, since I reckoned that their common sense would be indispensable to what I was undertaking. With us also was my son Adeodatus,

least of us all in age but whose intellectual aptitude, if my love does not deceive me, promises something great.

With all of them attentive, I began thus:

2.

7. "Does it seem obvious to you that we are composed of soul* and body?"[48]

When everyone agreed, Navigius replied that he did not know. I said to him, "Is it that you know* nothing at all, or is this particular matter to be numbered among some other things of which you are ignorant?"

"I don't reckon," he said, "that I'm ignorant of everything."

"Can you tell us one of the things that you do know?"

"I can," he said.

"Unless it would be a bother," I said, "give us one."

And while he was hesitating, I said, "Do you at least know* that you're alive?"[49]

"I do," he said.

"Then you know* that you have life, since no one can live unless it is by life."

"I know* that, too," he said.

"Do you also know* that you have a body?"

He agreed.

"Therefore, you already know* that you consist of a body and life."

"I do. At the same time, however, I'm uncertain whether these are the only two."

"Therefore," I said, "you don't doubt the existence of these two, the body and the soul*,[50] but you're uncertain whether there's something else that is capable of completing and perfecting a man."

"Yes," he said.

"If we can," I said, "we will inquire into what sort of thing this could be some other time.[51] Right now, since all of us acknowledge that a man can't exist without the body or the soul*, what I'm seeking from all of you is this: On account of which of these do we desire food?"

"On account of the body," said Licentius.

The others, however, were hesitating and holding various discussions among themselves on how it could be that food seems necessary for the body when it is desired on account of life, and life pertains to the soul* alone. Then I said, "Does it seem to you that food pertains to that part which we see growing and becoming more fit by means of food?"

All agreed except Trygetius. For he said, "Why haven't I grown in proportion to my voracious appetite?"

"All bodies," I said, "have their limit fixed by nature, beyond which measure they cannot proceed. Although these measures would decrease if there were insufficient nourishment (which we also notice rather easily in cattle), no one doubts that the bodies of all living things grow lean when food is taken away from them."

"To grow lean is not to grow less," Licentius said.

"It is sufficient," I said, "for what I want. As a matter of fact, the question is whether food pertains to the body. But it does pertain, since when food is withheld, the body is reduced to leanness."

All agreed that it was so.

8. "Then what about the soul*?" I said. "Is there a nourishment proper to it? Or does it seem to you that knowledge* is its food?"

"Obviously," Mother said. "I believe that the soul* is nourished by nothing other than the understanding and knowledge* of things."

When Trygetius showed that he had doubts about her statement, she said: "Didn't you yourself teach us today whence or where the soul* is fed? For only after taking some lunch did you say that you noticed what dish we were using, since you had been thinking about I don't know what else. And yet you didn't keep your hands and mouth away from that share of the food. So where was your mind at the time that it wasn't paying attention to what you were eating?[52] From this consideration, believe me that the mind is fed on courses such as these—that is, on its own theories and thoughts, provided that it can perceive something through them."

And after they noisily erupted with doubt about this point, I said, "Don't you concede that the minds of very learned men are much fuller and much greater in their own class, so to speak, than those of the unlearned?"

They said this was obvious.

"We therefore rightly say that the minds of those who haven't been educated by any of the disciplines and who haven't drunk deep of any of the fine arts[53] are hungry and famished, so to speak."

"I imagine," said Trygetius, "that their minds are full, but full of defects and worthlessness."

"That very thing," I said, "is a kind of barrenness and hunger, as it were, of the mind. For just as the body, when it is deprived of food, is frequently full of diseases and mange[54] (and these defects indicate starvation in the body), so too are their minds full of diseases by which they confess their hunger. As a matter of fact, the ancients considered 'worthlessness' [*nequitia*] itself,[55] which is the mother of all vices,[56] to be named from 'not anything' [*nec quicquam*], that is, from that which is nothing. And the virtue that is contrary to this vice is called frugality [*frugalitas*]. Just as this virtue is named after 'fruit' [*frux*], that is, after a 'fruitful enjoyment' [*fructus*]⁵⁷ on account of a certain fecundity of the mind, so too is worthlessness named after barrenness, that is, after nothing.[58] For 'nothing' is all that flows on, that is dissolved, that melts away, and that is ever being lost, so to speak—hence we also call men such as this lost.[59]

"But something *is* if it remains, if it stays constant, if it is always the same—as virtue is.[60] And a great and most beautiful part of virtue is what is called temperance and frugality. But if this is too obscure for you to see right now, you at least grant that if the minds of the unlearned are also full, then two kinds of nourishment are found with minds as well as with bodies: one salubrious and beneficial, the other unhealthy and harmful.

9. "Since this is the way things stand and because we are agreed that there are in man a certain 'two,' that is, a body and a soul*,[61] I imagine that on my birthday I ought to provide a meal a bit more sumptuous, one not only for our bodies, but for our souls* as well. Moreover, if you're hungry, I shall tell you what this meal is. For if you were unwilling and disdainful and I tried to feed you, I would expend effort in vain; instead, I should say prayers so that you may [one day] yearn for courses such as these rather than for those of the body. This will happen *if* your minds are healthy; since sick minds, as we see with diseases of the body itself, refuse their food and spit it out."[62]

By their very expressions and the approving tone in their voices, everyone said that they now wanted to accept and devour whatever it was I had prepared for them.

10. And I, in turn, began by saying, "We want to be happy."[63]

I had hardly gotten this out when they concurred, agreeing with one voice.

"Does it seem to you," I said, "that someone who doesn't have what he wants is happy?"

They said no.

"What?" I said. "Everyone who has what he wants is happy?"

Then Mother said, "If he wants good things and has them, he is happy; but if he wants bad things, he is unhappy, even if he has them."[64]

Laughing and jumping for joy,[65] I said to her: "Mother, you have utterly mastered the very citadel of philosophy.[66] No doubt words have failed you, so that you wouldn't be able to hold forth right now like Tully, whose words on this sentiment are the following. For in the *Hortensius*, a book he wrote in praise and defense of philosophy, he says: 'But behold, certainly not philosophers but those who are quick to argue say that everyone who lives as he himself wants to is happy. This, of course, is false; for to want what is not decent is itself the very worst misery. And not obtaining what you want is not so miserable as wanting to obtain what is not right, for depravity of the will brings more evil than fortune brings good to anyone.' "[67]

At these words Mother exclaimed in such a way that, thoroughly forgetting her sex, we thought that some great man was sitting with us.[68] In the meantime, I understood (insofar as I could) from what source and from how divine a source these things flowed.[69]

And then Licentius said, "But you ought to mention *what* someone should want in order to be happy and for what things it is right for him to have a desire."

"Invite me," I said, "on your birthday when you deign to do so, and I will gladly accept whatever you put on the table. On this condition, I ask that you feast with me today and not demand something that perhaps hasn't been prepared."

As he was regretting his modest and deferential suggestion, I said, "Then are we agreed that no one can be happy who doesn't have what he wants, nor can everyone who has what he wants be happy?"

They agreed.

11. "What about this?" I said. "Do you grant that everyone who isn't happy is miserable?"[70]

They had no doubt.

"Everyone, therefore," I said, "who doesn't have what he wants is miserable."

They all liked that.

"Then what should a man acquire for himself in order to be happy?" I said. "For perhaps this will also be served up at this banquet of ours, lest Licentius's keen appetite be neglected. For, I imagine, he should be able to acquire what he has whenever he wants it."[71]

They said this was obvious.

"Therefore," I said, "it should be something ever abiding and not dependent upon fortune or subject to any accidents. For we can't have whatever is mortal and perishable whenever we want it and for as long as we want it."[72]

Everyone agreed.

But Trygetius said, "There are many fortunate men who possess, abundantly and plentifully, those very things that are fragile and subject to accidents yet are pleasant for this life; nor do they lack any of the things they want."

I said to him, "Does it seem to you that someone who is afraid is happy?"

"No," he said.

"Then if someone can lose what he loves, is it possible for him *not* to be afraid?"[73]

"It isn't," he said.

"But these fortuitous things can be lost. Therefore, he who loves and possesses these things can't in any way be happy."

He disagreed with none of this.

At this point Mother said: "Even if he is secure [in the knowledge that] he isn't going to lose all these possessions, nevertheless, he couldn't be satisfied by things such as these. And therefore, he is miserable because he is forever wanting."

"What if," I said to her, "he abounds in all these things and is overflowing with them, but he places on himself a limit to his desires and is content to enjoy his possessions decently and pleasantly — doesn't he seem to you to be happy?"

"Then he's happy not by virtue of the things," she said, "but by virtue of the moderation of his mind."

"Excellent," I said. "This is the only answer that should be given to this question, and this is the only answer that you should give. Therefore, we don't doubt at all that if someone sets out to be happy, he should acquire for himself that which abides forever and can't be taken away from him by any cruel act of fortune."

"We agreed to this a little while ago," Trygetius said.

"Does it seem to you," I said, "that God is eternal and ever abiding?"

"Of course He is," Licentius said. "This is so certain that there's no need for an inquiry."

All the others agreed with pious devotion.

"Then he who has God," I said, "is happy."[74]

12. When they joyfully and most gladly accepted this, I said: "Then I imagine that we should now be seeking nothing else but who out of all men has God; for surely, *he* will be happy. I seek to learn your opinion about him."

Here Licentius said, "He has God who lives well."

Trygetius said, "He has God who does what God wants done."

Lartidianus agreed with his opinion. But the boy, the youngest of them all,[75] said, "He has God who doesn't have an unclean spirit."

Mother certainly approved of them all but especially this one.

Navigius was silent, and when I asked him what he thought, he replied that he liked the last one.

And it did not seem proper to neglect asking Rusticus what, pray tell, his opinion was on so great a matter (it seemed to me that he was keeping quiet because he was hampered not so much by deliberation as by shyness). He agreed with Trygetius.

13. Then I said: "I [now] have a hold on everyone's opinion concerning this very great matter. If only we could investigate it as we began, with the utmost serenity and sincerity, it wouldn't be necessary for us to seek, nor could we find, anything beyond it. But it's late in the day and souls can also be excessive in their courses if they rush into them voraciously and beyond measure, and thus there's a way in which they suffer from indigestion. (Thus, for the sake of our minds'* health, we should dread this condition no less than starvation itself.)[76] Hence, if it's alright with you, this question will treat us better tomorrow when we are hungry. For now, I would like you to relish what has suddenly suggested itself to the mind* of me, your waiter, as something I should bring out (since things of this sort are usually served last), something that is, unless I'm mistaken, made up and seasoned with scholastic honey."

When they heard this, they all lunged for the dish being carried in, so to speak, and compelled me to hurry up and tell them what in the world it could be.

"What do you think it is?" I said. "Unless you think this whole business with the Academics that we undertook is over."[77]

As soon as the three who knew about this took in the name, they rose up quite eagerly;[78] and, just as if they were helping a server with their outstretched hands (as is often the case), they demonstrated with whatever words they could that there was nothing they would enjoy hearing more.

14. Then, I put the matter this way: "If it is obvious," I said, "that someone who doesn't have what he wants isn't happy, which our reasoning demonstrated a little while ago;[79] but no one seeks what he doesn't want to find, and they [the Academics] are always seeking the truth and therefore want to find it (and thus want to 'have' a discovery of the truth) but don't—then it follows that [the Academics] don't have what they want, and from this it also follows that they aren't happy. But no one is wise unless he is happy;[80] therefore, the Academic is not wise."

Here they suddenly cried out, as if they were snatching up [the treat] whole. But Licentius, who was very diligently and carefully paying attention, was afraid of agreeing. He thus submitted the following: "Yes, I snatched this up along with you since indeed I was moved by that conclusion and cried out. But from now on, I will admit nothing into my innards[81] and will save my portion for Alypius; for he will either slurp it up along with me or advise me as to why it shouldn't be touched."[82]

"With his bad spleen,[83] Navigius should be more afraid of sweets," I said.

Here, laughing, [Navigius] said: "Clearly, things such as these will cure me. For what you have set before us—somehow tangled as well as prickly—is, as that famous man says of Hymettic honey, bittersweet.[84] And it doesn't bloat my innards at all! And so after taking a little taste, I'm still most gladly cramming all of it down, as much as I can, into the marrow [of my being]. For I don't see how this conclusion of yours can be refuted."

"There's no way at all it can be!" Trygetius said. "Therefore I rejoice now that I took up arms against [the Academics] a while ago.[85] For even though I was ignorant of how they could be refuted, I was still very much opposed to them, either by some unknown impulse of nature or, to speak more truly, by God."

15. Here Licentius said, "I for one am not deserting them yet."

"Then you disagree with us?" Trygetius asked.

"What in the world?" Licentius said. "You all disagree with Alypius?"

"I have no doubt that if Alypius were here," I said to him, "he would yield to this succinct bit of reasoning.[86] For he wouldn't [possibly] think in such absurd ways: that it would seem to him that someone who doesn't have so great a good of the soul [i.e., the truth], which he most ardently wants to have, is happy; or that they [the Academics] don't want to discover the truth; or that he who isn't happy is wise. For what you're afraid of tasting is made up of these three ingredients—honey, flour, and nuts, so to speak."

"Would *he* yield," he said, "to so small a schoolboy lure and abandon the great abundance of the Academics, an abundance that could flood this little whatever-it-is and either drown it or drag it on?"

"As if indeed," I said, "we are seeking something long, especially against Alypius; for from his own body he proves well enough for himself that those things which are small are in no small way strong and useful. But as for you who have chosen to depend on the authority of someone who is absent, of which of these [statements] do you not approve? That he is not happy who doesn't have what he wants? Or that they deny wanting to have a discovery of the truth, into which they are vehemently inquiring? Or that it seems to you that someone who is wise isn't happy?"

"The man who doesn't have what he wants," he said, laughing testily, "is totally happy."[87]

When I gave instructions for this to be written down, he cried out, saying, "I didn't say that!"

When I again gave the nod for it to be written down, he said, "I said it."

And I ordered once and for all that no word fall outside the records. In this way I kept that youngster all worked up between shame and consistency.

16. But when we were jokingly provoking him with these words to eat his share, so to speak, I noticed that the others were staring at us without laughing, for they were unaware of the whole affair and were keen to know* what was so pleasantly going on among just [the four of] us. It seemed to me that they were very much like those who, when they feast with extremely insatiable and ravenous banqueters (and this happens frequently), either refrain from being rapacious out of a sense of dignity or are deterred from becoming rapacious out of a sense of shyness.[88] And because I myself had invited them and because you have taught me how to play the role of some great man (of a real man, to explain it thoroughly) and even how to play the summoner at these feasts, this inequality and discrepancy at our table disturbed me.[89] I smiled at Mother. She was only too glad to command that what they had less of should be brought forth as if it were from her very own cellar, and so she said: "Tell us now, and give us an account of who these Academics of yours are and what they have in mind."

When I briefly and clearly explained it to her in such a way that no one might go away ignorant of them, she said, "These men of yours are spazzes!"—a name commonly given among us to those who suffer from the falling sickness.[90]

She rose at once to leave; and here, after bringing our conversation to an end, all of us departed, joyful and laughing.

3.

17. The next day, likewise after lunch but a little later than the day before, when the same people had taken their seats in the same place, I said: "You have come late to the banquet, which I imagine has happened not because of indigestion but because of your assurance that there would be a paucity of courses. And because you reckoned that you would be gobbling these courses up quickly, it seemed best not to bother approaching [the table] so early. In fact, you had figured that there wouldn't be many leftovers remaining from a day and from a celebration in which the fare was, as you discovered, so meager!

"Perhaps you're right. But like you, I don't know what has been prepared for you. For there's someone else who does not cease to provide all dishes, especially such excellent dishes as these, and yet we frequently stop eating either because of weakness or satiety or business. He is the one who, dwelling in men, makes them happy (and if I'm not mistaken, we all piously and resolutely agreed on this yesterday).[91] For when reason had demonstrated that someone who has God is happy and none of you had opposed this opinion, it was asked who in the world seemed to you to have God. And if I remember correctly, you expressed three opinions on the matter. For several liked [the definition] that he who does what God wishes has God; some, however, said that he who lives well has God; but for the rest, God seemed to be in those in whom there is not what is called an unclean spirit.

18. "But perhaps all of you have sensed one and the same thing but [have articulated it] with different words. For, if we consider the first two statements—everyone who lives well does the things that God wants and everyone who does the things that God wants lives well—[then we realize that] living well is nothing else but

doing the things that please God. Unless it seems to you to be otherwise."

They agreed.

"But that third statement must be considered a little more diligently on account of the fact that in the rite of the most pure sacred ceremonies, insofar as I understand it, it is the custom to speak of an unclean spirit in two different ways.[92] Either it is that which goes into a soul* from the outside and disturbs the senses and inflicts a certain madness on men.[93] In order to remove it, the presiders are said to impose hands or to exorcize, that is, drive it out by adjuring it with the help of the divine.[94] Or otherwise, every soul* that is in any way 'unclean'—which means nothing else than being stained by vices or errors—is called an unclean spirit.

"Therefore, I ask you, boy, you who perhaps proffered that opinion in a somewhat more serene and purified spirit—who is it that seems to you not to have an unclean spirit: he who does not have a demon, by which men usually become deranged, or he who has already cleansed his soul* from all vices and sins?"

"It seems to me," [Adeodatus] said, "that he who lives chastely does not have an unclean spirit."

"But whom do you call chaste?" I asked. "He who commits no sin, or he who refrains from illicit intercourse?"

"How can he be chaste," he said, "when, abstaining only from illicit intercourse, he doesn't stop from being stained by the other sins? He is truly chaste who pays attention to God and holds himself to Him alone."

When I decided to have the boy's words written down [exactly] as they were spoken,[95] I said, "Therefore, it is necessary for him to live well, and he who lives well is necessarily such a man—unless it seems to you otherwise."

He conceded that, along with the others.

"Therefore," I said, "there is but one opinion expressed here.

19. "But for a little while now, I ask you all this: Does God want man to seek God?"[96]

They granted that.

"Again I ask: can we, pray tell, say that he who seeks God lives badly?"

"No way," they said.

"Answer this third question as well: Can an unclean spirit seek God?"

They said it could not. Navigius, who was somewhat hesitant, eventually yielded to the others' voices.

"If, therefore," I said, "he who seeks God does what God wants, he both lives well and doesn't have an unclean spirit. But he who seeks God doesn't yet have God. Therefore, we shouldn't necessarily say that whoever either lives well or does what God wants or doesn't have an unclean spirit has God."

Here, as the others were laughing at themselves for having been duped by their own concessions, Mother, who had been dumbfounded for a while, asked that I untangle and loosen for her this thing by explaining what I had verbally twisted by dint of a syllogistic conclusion.[97] When this had been done, she said, "But nobody can reach God unless he seeks God."

"Excellent," I said. "Nevertheless, he who still seeks hasn't yet reached God; plus, he is already living well. Therefore, it is not [necessarily the case] that whoever lives well has God."

"It seems to me," she said, "that everyone has God, but those who live well have God well-disposed to them, while those who live badly have God hostile to them."

"Then yesterday," I said, "we conceded poorly that he who has God is happy,[98] if indeed every man has God and yet not every man is happy."

"Then add 'well-disposed,' " she said.

20. "Are we at least sufficiently certain," I said, "that he is happy who has God well-disposed to him?"

"I would like to agree," Navigius said, "but I fear for [the case of] the man who is still seeking, especially lest you go on to conclude that the Academic is happy. Indeed, during yesterday's discussion, the Academic was designated—in lowbrow and bad Latin to be sure, but certainly with a most appropriate word, it seems to me—a 'spazz.'[99] For I can't say that God is against a man who is seeking God. But if it's wrong to say this, then [God] will be well-disposed to him, and he who has God well-disposed to him is happy. Therefore, he who seeks God will be happy. However, everyone who is seeking doesn't yet have what he wants; therefore, the happy man will be someone who doesn't have what he wants. But such a conclusion seemed absurd to us all yesterday, which is why we believed that the darkness of the Academics had been dispelled.[100] Therefore, Licentius will now triumph over us, and like a prudent physician he will admonish me that those sweets, which I rashly took against the better interests of my health, are exacting this punishment from me."[101]

21. Here, when even Mother was laughing, Trygetius said: "I don't necessarily grant that God is against the man to whom He isn't well-disposed; but there is, I reckon, something in between."

So I said to him, "Yet you grant that that man of yours in the middle, to whom God is neither well-disposed nor hostile, somehow has God?"

Here, while he was delaying, Mother said, "It is one thing to have God, another not to be without God."

"What, therefore, is better?" I asked: "to have God or not to be without God?"

"Insofar as I can understand it," she said, "this is my opinion: He who lives well has God, but God is well-disposed to him; he who lives badly has God, but God is against him. However, he who is still seeking God and hasn't yet found Him has [God] neither well-disposed to him nor against him, but he is not without God."

I said to the others, "Is this also your opinion?"

They said that it was.

"Tell me," I said, "does it not seem to you that God is well-disposed to the man whom He favors?"

They admitted that this was so.

"Then does God not favor," I asked, "the man who is seeking Him?"

They replied that He *does* favor him.

"Therefore," I said, "he who is seeking God has God well-disposed to him, and everyone who has God well-disposed to him is happy. Therefore, he who seeks is also happy. However, he who is seeking doesn't yet have what he wants; and thus, he who doesn't have what he wants will be happy."

"In no way does it seem to me," Mother said, "that he who doesn't have what he wants is happy."

"Then not everyone who has God well-disposed to him is happy," I said.

"If reason compels this conclusion," she said, "I can't deny it."

"Then this will be our distinction," I said: "Everyone who already has God has God well-disposed to him and is happy; but everyone who is seeking God has God well-disposed to him and isn't yet happy. Moreover, whoever is alienating himself from God by vices and sins is not only not happy, but he doesn't even live with God well-disposed to him."

22. When everyone found this agreeable, I said: "Very well, but I still fear that what we had granted above may disturb you—that

whoever isn't happy is miserable,[102] from which it will follow that a man is miserable who [seeks God, even when God is well-disposed to him]. [The rest of the paragraph, which is missing from all extant manuscripts, continues with this theme.][103]

[An entire paragraph is missing.]

[The next paragraph, the opening half of which is missing, probably develops the theme of need or being needy. It resumes with] ". . . someone happy. As Tully says, 'Or indeed, do we call the lords of many estates throughout the land rich, and shall we name the possessors of all virtues poor?'[104]

"But consider this: whether, just as it is true that every person in need is miserable, so too is it true that every miserable person is in need. For in this way it will be true that misery is nothing else but need—which, as you can now tell as it's being said, is [a position] I approve of. But it's too late in the day for us to continue seeking. Consequently, lest you develop a distaste for this, I ask that we meet at this table of ours tomorrow as well."

When all had said that they would most gladly do so, we arose.

4.

23. But on the third day of our disputation, the morning clouds that had been forcing us into the baths dispersed, and the season gave us back a crystal clear afternoon.[105] Hence we decided to go down to the part of the little meadow that was nearby, and once everyone had taken a seat where it seemed comfortable, the remainder of our discussion was completed thus: "I have and am holding," I said, "almost all the things that I wanted you to concede when I questioned you. And so today, there won't be anything or much (as I see it) to necessitate your answering me, thereby finally

enabling us to round off our banquet by a certain span of days. For Mother had said that misery is nothing other than need, and we agreed that all who are in need are miserable.[106] But whether all who are miserable are also in need is one question that we weren't able to unpack yesterday.

"If, however, reason demonstrates that this is so, then we will most perfectly discover who is happy, for it will be he who isn't in need. For everyone who isn't miserable is happy;[107] therefore, he who is without need is happy if it is established that what we are calling need is the same as misery."

24. "What objection can be made to that?" Trygetius said. "Can't it already be concluded that every man who is not in need is happy from the obvious fact that every man who is in need is miserable? For I recall that we conceded that there's no middle ground between being miserable and being happy."[108]

"Does it seem to you," I said, "that there is any middle ground between being a dead man and being a live one? Isn't it true that every man is either living or dead?"

"I acknowledge that there's no middle ground here," he said, "but where are you going with this?"

"Because," I said, "I believe that you will also acknowledge that every man who was buried a year ago is dead."

He did not deny it.

"What?" I said. "Everyone who wasn't buried a year ago is alive?"

"That doesn't follow," he said.

"Therefore," I said, "it doesn't follow that if everyone who is in need is miserable, everyone who isn't in need is happy—even though no middle ground can be found between being miserable and being happy, as none can be found between being alive and being dead."

25. Since some of them understood [this argument] a little more slowly, I unpacked it and turned it over and over as best I could with words accommodated to their sense of things.

"Therefore," I said, "no one doubts that every man who is in need is miserable; nor are we intimidated by certain things necessary for the body of wise men. For the soul itself, in which the happy life is situated,[109] has no need of them, since it is perfect, and nothing is perfect that is in need of something. The soul will, however, take what is apparently necessary for the body if it's at hand. If it isn't, a lack of these things won't break it. In fact, every wise man is strong, and no strong man is afraid of anything. Therefore, the wise man doesn't fear either the death of the body or the pains that are to be gotten rid of, avoided, or deferred by those necessities that are susceptible to becoming scarce for him.[110] Nevertheless, if these goods are available, he won't stop using them well, for the statement, 'It is foolish to let in what you can avoid,'[111] is very, very true.

"Therefore, [the wise man] will avoid death and pain, insofar as he can and insofar as it is proper, lest in avoiding nothing at all he becomes miserable—not because these things are happening to him but because he didn't avoid them when he could have, which is an obvious sign of folly. Thus, the person who doesn't avoid these things will be miserable not from enduring them, but from folly. But if he isn't able to avoid these things when they rush upon him, even though his conduct has been careful and decent, they won't make him miserable. For that statement of the same comic is no less true: 'Since what you want can't be done, wish for what you can do.'[112] How will someone be miserable to whom nothing happens against his will, since he can't wish for that which he sees cannot befall him? For he has his will [set on] the most certain of things; that is, whatever he does, he does only by some precept of virtue and by the divine law of wisdom, which in no way can be taken away from him.[113]

26. "Now then, consider whether everyone who is miserable is also in need. For something makes it difficult to grant this statement—the fact that many have been placed in a great abundance of fortuitous possessions, for whom everything is so easy that whatever they crave[114] is available at their beck and call.[115] This life of theirs is difficult indeed! But let's nevertheless imagine someone who is the same kind of man that Tully says Orata was.[116] For who would easily say that Orata was distressed by need, a man who was extremely wealthy, extremely charming, extremely discriminating, and who lacked nothing with respect to pleasure, influence, and good and vigorous health? For he abounded in the most lucrative estates and the most delightful friends, as much as he wanted; and all of these things he used most suitably for the health of the body. And to make a long story short, prosperous success followed his every plan and his every wish.

"But perhaps one of you will say that he wanted to have more than he did. We don't know this. However, and this is sufficient for our inquiry, let's suppose that he did not desire more than he had. Does he seem to you to be in need?"

"Even if," Licentius said, "I concede that he desired nothing more (and I don't know how I would accept this about a man who isn't wise)—still, he must have been afraid that all these possessions would be snatched away from him by even a single adverse blow, since it is said that he was a man of no mean intelligence. Indeed, it was no big deal [for him] to understand that all such things, no matter how great, are subject to chance."

Then, smiling, I said: "You see, Licentius, that this most fortunate man of ours was kept from the happy life by the keenness of his intelligence.[117] For the more astute he was, the more he saw that he could lose all those things. He was crushed by this fear, and clearly enough did he confirm that common adage: 'The treacherous man is wise about his own evil.' "[118]

27. Here, when he and the others smiled, I said: "Yet let's attend to this more carefully, since even if this man of ours was afraid, he wasn't in need—hence our question. For being in need consists in not having, not in the fear of losing what you do have. But this man of ours was miserable because he was afraid, although he wasn't in need. Therefore, not everyone who is miserable is in need."

Although she whose opinion I was defending also approved of this along with the others,[119] she was nevertheless somewhat hesitant.

"I still don't know," she said, "and I still don't understand clearly how misery can be separated from need or need from misery. For this man of ours, who was rich and wealthy, desired nothing more, as you say. Still, because he was afraid that he would lose [his possessions], he was in need of wisdom. If he had needed silver and money, would we not then call him needy? Shall we not call it need when he needs wisdom?"

Here, when all cried out with wonder, I myself was also not a little bit delighted and glad that she had said the most powerful thing, which, as a great thing from the books of the philosophers,[120] I had planned to bring out last.

"Do you all see," I said, "that a myriad of various doctrines is one thing, a mind utterly attentive to God, another?[121] For where did these words that filled us with wonder come from if not from there?"

"Absolutely," Licentius joyfully cried out here. "Nothing truer, nothing more divine can be said. For there is no need greater and more miserable than the need for wisdom, and someone who doesn't need wisdom cannot need anything at all."

28. "Then neediness of the mind," I said, "is nothing else but folly. For this is the opposite of wisdom, and it is opposite in the same way that death is opposed to life and the happy life is opposed to misery—that is, without any middle ground in between. For just as every man who isn't happy is miserable and every man who isn't dead is alive, so too is it obvious that everyone who isn't a fool is wise. Hence we may now see that Sergius Orata was miserable not only because he feared losing the gifts of fortune, but because he was a fool. And hence it is the case that he would have been more miserable if he had not fretted at all for such wavering uncertainties, which he reckoned to be good. For he would have had more assurance not by his courage keeping guard, but by his mind dozing off, and, sunk deep in an [even] deeper folly, he would have been miserable.[122] But if everyone who lacks wisdom suffers great need, and everyone in possession of wisdom needs nothing, it follows that folly is need. However, as every fool is miserable, so too is every miserable person a fool.[123] Therefore, as every need is misery, so too has it been proved that every misery is need."

29. When Trygetius said that he did not sufficiently understand this conclusion, I said, "On what did we agree through our reasoning?"

"That someone who doesn't have wisdom is in need," he said.

"Then what is it to be in need?" I asked.

"Not having wisdom," he said.

"What is not having wisdom?" I asked.

Here, when he was silent, I said, "Isn't it having folly?"

"It is," he said.

"Therefore," I said, "having need is nothing else but having folly; hence it is necessarily the case that 'need' is being called by another name any time that it's called 'folly.' Although, I don't know how we can say 'he has need' or 'he has folly.' For it's the same kind of thing as saying that some place which lacks light 'has darkness,' which means nothing else than that it doesn't have light. For it's not as if darkness comes or goes, but that 'to lack light' is itself to be dark just now, just as 'to lack clothing' is to be naked. For nakedness doesn't run away at the approach of clothing as if it were something mobile. So, therefore, we say that someone has need as if we were saying that he has nakedness, for 'need' is a word for 'not having.'

"Therefore, to explain what I mean as well as I can, 'he has need' is said in such a way as if it were being said, 'he has not having.' And thus, if it has been shown that folly is itself a true and definite need, consider now whether the question that we took up has been resolved. For there was some doubt among us as to whether what we've been calling misery is nothing else than what we've been calling need.[124] However, we have now given a reason why folly is rightly called need. Therefore, just as every fool is miserable and every miserable man is a fool, so too must we acknowledge that not only is everyone who is in need miserable, but also that everyone who is miserable is in need. But if we deduce that folly is misery from the [propositions] that every fool is miserable and every miserable man a fool, then why do we not deduce that misery is nothing else but need from the [propositions] that whoever is in need is miserable and whoever is miserable is in need?"

30. When all had acknowledged this to be so, I said: "It now follows that we consider who is not in need, for he will be wise and happy.[125] Folly is need and a name for need, but this word ['need'] usually signifies a certain barrenness and lack. Pay very close attention, I beseech, to the great care with which the ancients created either all or, which is obvious, some words, especially words for those things it was very necessary to be familiar with. For now you concede that every fool is in need and everyone who is in need is

a fool; I also believe you concede that a foolish soul is vice-laden and that all of the soul's vices are included in the one name 'folly.'[126] Moreover, on the first day of our disputation we had said that worthlessness [*nequitia*] is said to be from that which is not anything [*nec quicquam*], and that its opposite, frugality [*frugalitas*], is named after fruit [*frux*].[127] Therefore, in these two opposites, that is, in frugality and worthlessness, the following two seem to stand out: being and nonbeing.[128] What, however, do we reckon is the opposite of need, which is the source of our question?"

Here, after they dallied for a short while, Trygetius said, "If I were to say wealth, I would see that poverty is its opposite."

"That certainly is close," I said, "for poverty and need are usually taken to be one and the same. Nevertheless, another word should be found, lest the superior side be lacking a noun. Otherwise, while the other side abounds with the names 'poverty' and 'need,' the name 'wealth' is the only one opposed to them on this side. For nothing is more absurd than the need for a noun that is the counterpart to 'need.' "

" 'Fullness,' if I may say so," Licentius said, "seems to me to be the correct opposite of 'need.' "

31. "Perhaps we can inquire into this word a little more carefully later on," I said, "for this is not of vital concern in our [current] search for the truth. For although Sallust, a most excellent weigher of words, made 'opulence' the opposite of 'need,' I still accept that 'fullness' of yours.[129] Indeed, we'll be free from the terror of the grammarians in this place, nor should we fear being chastised for using words nonchalantly by those who have given us their property to use."[130]

At which point, after they had smiled, I said: "Because your minds*, when you're intent on God, are like certain oracles, I have decided not to disregard them.[131] And so let's see what this term means; for I imagine that none is better suited to the truth. 'Fullness' and 'need,' then, are opposites;[132] but even here, as in 'worthlessness' and 'frugality,' there likewise appear those two, being and nonbeing.[133] And, if need is folly itself, fullness will be wisdom.

"Many have also said that frugality is the mother of all virtues,[134] and rightly so. Agreeing with them Tully even said in a well-known speech, 'Let each man take it as he will; yet as for me, I judge frugality, that is, moderation and temperance, to be the greatest virtue.'[135]

"He said this in a most learned and appropriate way, for he was considering 'fruit' [*frux*] — that is, what we are calling 'being' [*esse*], the opposite of which is 'nonbeing' [*non esse*].[136] But on account of the common usage of speech, in which frugality is usually spoken of as if it were [synonymous with] stinginess, he illustrated what he meant with the help of two qualifications: he added 'moderation' and 'temperance.' And it is these two words to which we should pay more careful attention.

32. "In particular, 'moderation' [*modestia*] is said to come from 'measure' [*modus*][137] and 'temperance' [*temperantia*] from 'right mixture' [*temperies*]. Moreover, where there is measure and right mixture, there is nothing more, nothing less. It is much better, therefore, that we set up fullness itself [*plenitudo*] as the opposite of need rather than giving the position to abundance [*abundantia*]. For by 'abundance' is understood 'affluence' [*affluentia*], as if there were an outpouring of something gushing out excessively.[138] When this happens beyond that which is sufficient, there's also a need for measure [*modus*]; and the thing that is excessive stands in need of a limit [*modus*]. Need, therefore, is no stranger to a very overflow [*redundantia*], but both 'more' and 'less' are strangers to measure. Also, if you analyze opulence itself, you will find that it contains nothing other than measure, for 'opulence' [*opulentia*] is said to come from no other place but 'riches' [*ops*]. But how does that

which is too much enrich [*opitulor*], since too much is often more troublesome than too little? Whatever, therefore, is either too much or too little is liable to need because it is in need of measure.

"The measure of the mind, then, is wisdom. In fact, we don't deny that wisdom is the opposite of folly and that folly is need, and yet fullness is the opposite of need. Wisdom, therefore, is fullness. Moreover, in fullness there is measure, and thus the mind's measure is in wisdom.[139] Hence that illustrious [adage] which is rightly known both far and wide: 'In life, the first advantageous principle is this: nothing to excess.'[140]

33. "We had said, however, at the beginning of our disputation today that if we discovered that misery was nothing else but need, we would acknowledge that he is happy who isn't in need.[141] And now it has been discovered. Therefore, to be happy is nothing else but not to be in need, that is, to be wise. If, however, we inquire into what wisdom is, reason has already opened this up and brought it out, insofar as it could at the present time. For wisdom is none other than the measure of the mind, that is, that by which the mind balances itself, the result being that it neither runs over into excess nor is it constricted by what is less than full. On one hand, the mind runs over into luxuries, despotisms, acts of pride, and the other things of this kind by which the minds of immoderate and miserable men reckon that they will be procuring for themselves joy and power. On the other, it is constricted by baseness, fear, sorrow, desire,[142] and whatever other things through which even miserable men admit that they are miserable.

"But when [the mind] contemplates the wisdom that has been discovered and, to use this boy's term, holds itself to [wisdom],[143] and when, being undisturbed by any inane thing, it turns not to the mirage of images[144] (embracing the weight of which it is inclined to fall from its God and sink),[145] it fears no immoderation and thence no need and thus no misery. Whoever is happy, therefore, has his own measure, that is, wisdom.

34. "But what is to be called wisdom other than the wisdom of God? We have also learned by divine authority, however, that the Son of God is none other than the Wisdom of God,[146] and the Son of God is surely God. Therefore, whoever is happy has God, which we all determined previously when we began this banquet.[147] But what do you reckon wisdom is if not the truth? For it has also been said, "I am the Truth."[148] In order for it to exist, truth arises through some supreme measure[149] from which it proceeds and into which it is converted, once it is perfected. No other measure, however, is placed upon the supreme measure itself; for if the supreme measure is a measure by virtue of supreme measure, it is measure by virtue of itself.[150] But it is necessary even for the supreme measure that it be a true measure. Thus, as truth is begotten from measure, so too is measure learned from the truth.[151] And thus, there is never truth without measure or measure without truth.[152] Who is the Son of God? It has been said: "Truth." Who is it that has no father? Who other than the Supreme Measure? Whoever, therefore, comes to the Supreme Measure through the Truth is happy. For souls, this is 'having God,' that is, thoroughly enjoying God. For the rest, although they are had by God, they don't have God.

35. "Moreover, a certain Admonition that pleads with us to remember God, to seek Him, and—after driving out all distaste—to thirst for Him flows out to us from the very Font of Truth.[153] This secret sun pours forth its radiance into our interior lamps.[154] To it belongs everything true that we utter, even when, with eyes that are less than healthy or suddenly opened,[155] we're scared of

being boldly turned around and beholding the whole.[156] And this [light] also appears to be none other than God, perfect without the impediment of any corruption.[157] For there it is wholly and all perfect, and at the same time it is the most almighty God. But while we are still seeking, let's admit that we haven't yet been filled up by that Font itself and—to use the word—by fullness, and that we haven't yet reached our measure. And therefore, although God is now helping us, we are nevertheless not yet wise and happy. This, then, is the full satisfaction of souls, this is the happy life: to know piously and perfectly Him by whom you are led to the Truth, whereby you may thoroughly enjoy the Truth, through which you may be joined to the Supreme Measure.[158] These three show one God and one substance to the intelligent, provided that the vanities of various superstitions have been cast out."

Here, Mother, remembering the words that were fixed deep in her memory and awakening to her faith, as it were, joyfully poured forth the verse of our priest, "Cherish, O Trinity, those who pray."[159]

Then she added: "Without doubt, this is the happy life, the life that is perfect. And we must presume that we who are hurrying to it can be brought to it by a firm faith, a lively hope, and an ardent charity."[160]

36. "Therefore," I said, "because measure itself admonishes us to mark off our banquet by a certain span of days,[161] with all my might[162] I thank the supreme and true God the Father, the Lord, the liberator of souls*. And next, I thank you all who, once cordially invited, have also heaped many gifts upon me. For you've brought so much to our discussion that I cannot deny that I have been sated by my own guests!"

Here, when everyone was rejoicing and praising God, Trygetius said, "How I wish that you would feed us this way[163] every day."

"This measure," I said, "should be everywhere kept, everywhere loved, if our return to God is dear to your hearts."[164]

And with these words, our disputation came to an end and we departed.

Finis.

COMMENTARY

THE COVER LETTER (1.1–6)
Taking Sail Against a Sea of Troubles (1.1–2)

In offering an extended nautical metaphor involving philosophy and the vicissitudes of life, Augustine is reprising a theme that he has already explored in the two cover letters of *Against the Academics*, the prequel to *On the Happy Life*. In both dialogues, Augustine stresses that philosophy and the life of virtue it entails are essential to happiness and that fortune or luck and the things that depend on it, however so slightly, cannot be an essential component of the happy life. Wealth, bodily health, honor or success, the affairs of the heart—all of these are to some extent products of good fortune and therefore vulnerable to misfortune. Therefore, building one's happiness on these vulnerable goods is building one's house on sand. As Augustine writes, "Those who are dominated by fortune are those whom fortune puts in second place" (1.5).

Fortune's false appearances promising happiness are seductive, especially when one is being tossed to and fro on a "stormy sea" (1.1). This tumult often leads to a desire to control or manipulate fortune—to maximize the fortune one thinks is good and to minimize the misfortune one thinks is bad. The result is that one's attention becomes more consumed by the question of how to ride the waves to one's advantage than by the more important question of how to become immune to their effects or rise above them altogether.

And yet, if fortune is the problem, it can also initiate the solution. Augustine holds—and here he differs from philosophical predecessors like Cicero—that the path to philosophy, which ultimately renders one immune from fortune, always begins with a stroke of fortune.[1] Cicero's growth in virtue or wisdom, for example, may have never begun had he not chanced upon the study of philosophy when he was young; and Plato may never have become a lover of wisdom had he not met Socrates. Such is the case for "unfortunate" events as well, which, Augustine states, only the foolish label "adverse." Incidents of illness, financial or legal trouble, dishonor, the death of a loved one, and so forth undoubtedly cause pain and hardship, but they can also lead one to the realization that it is better to pursue wisdom and virtue (which are beyond the reach of fickle fortune) than goods like money, health, and marriage (which are not). Sometimes, in order to escape the stormy sea once and for all, one needs a good storm.

Augustine's use of a ship in distress as an example of good misfortune has a long philosophical pedigree. After surviving a shipwreck, the philosopher Aristippus is said to have remarked, "Children ought to be furnished with the kinds of possessions and provisions that can swim with them as one, even out of a shipwreck."[2] According to legend, the founder of Stoicism, Zeno of Citium, turned to philosophy after the ship he was on sank off the coast of Athens and he chanced upon a copy of Xenophon's *Memorabilia*. Years later he would say, "I now find that I made a prosperous voyage when I was shipwrecked."[3]

An Augustinian Geography (1.2–3)

Augustine's nautical chart is also a common device in philosophical literature, but he has added two novelties. The open sea as a metaphor for a life dominated by fortune is not new, nor is the image of philosophy as a port that enables one to escape definitively from the troublesome sea. Entering the port of philosophy does not mean that one will never again be struck by fortune or misfortune; it means that one has gained the wherewithal, in the form of genuine intellectual and moral virtue, never to be disturbed by reverses in fortune, however extreme these may be.

Yet as important as this immunity from fortune-induced anxiety is, it is not happiness. Augustine's first change to the map is the greater stress he places on the dry land that lies beyond the port of philosophy. The philosophical life is instrumental in acquiring happiness, but it is the means rather than the end, a necessary condition perhaps, but not a sufficient one. This more critical view of the limits of philosophy differs from Cicero's statement in *On Duties* that philosophy sees *and* enables the happy life, and that if philosophy cannot do this, nothing can (2.2.6). Augustine, on the other hand, not only distinguishes philosophy from the happy life, but he never portrays anyone dwelling firmly on the dry land of bliss: even Manlius Theodorus, the Christian Neoplatonic intellectual to whom he dedicates the dialogue, is described as only "clinging" to the land (1.5).

Moreover, Augustine describes the port of philosophy as "wide open," unable to keep out every error (1.5). The philosophers, despite their excellence, are not infallible; something more than pure philosophy is therefore needed. Augustine opines that the port's "vastness is now less dangerous," but he does not explain what he means by this statement. His positive assessment of contemporary philosophy may tie in to his view that Neoplatonism, with its strong reassertion of the distinction between sensible and intelligible reality, marks an advancement over the inconclusive dithering of the Academics;[4] or perhaps it is a reference to the purported purification of Neoplatonism by illustrious Christian thinkers such as Ambrose and Theodorus.[5]

The second change to the map is the "vast mountain" in front of the port, which Augustine identifies as "the proud zeal for utterly empty glory" (1.3). This mountain is similar to the mountain of Academic skepticism that Augustine criticizes elsewhere as blocking the way of those entering into philosophy,[6] but its meaning is broader. The mountain symbolizes pride in one's knowledge, which is why its terrain is described as volcanic; for just as knowledge without humility or charity artificially "puffs up" rather than genu- inely "edifies" the sinner (1 Cor 8:1), so too does a volcanic eruption expand the surface in a way that is unstable and deadly.

Who is on this mountain? As we have mentioned, the Academics have been implicated, and it may also be a veiled warning to Theodorus not to let his worldly success go to his head. But more generally, the mountain is host to all those who try to capitalize on philosophy for the sake of personal glory or recogni- tion. As the love of wisdom, philosophy is a perfectly shareable good: its aim is the attainment of the infinitely shareable prize that is wisdom,[7] and even the activity itself is perfectly shareable, for one person's philosophizing does not mean that there is less philoso- phizing left for another. True, philosophy is something that only a small minority of human beings ever do well, but this is more of a comment on the fallen nature of humankind than on the nature of philosophy per se. It is precisely because philosophy is such a shareable good that its exploitation for personal gain or its serving as the occasion for boastfulness is especially odious. One of the chief benefits of philosophy is its freedom from the often destructive cycle of competition over goods that are not completely shareable (money, honor, bragging rights, etc.).[8] When, therefore, philosophers philosophize in order to stand apart from the rest of the crowd and make a name for themselves, they are turning a love of the shareable into a competition over the unshareable, since they are now vying not for truth, but for honor and recognition, of which there is only so much to go around. They are like Alexander the Great, who chided his tutor Aristotle for publishing the *Metaphysics* on the grounds that there would be less glory for him if everyone knew the same secret doctrines as he—a comment that reveals Alexander to be a better general than philosopher.[9] In Augustine's metaphor the mountain dwellers enjoy looking down on everyone else, and although they are responsible for luring people away from the port toward the mountain, they also deter others from climbing it by stressing the difficulty of the ascent. It is as if they were reluctant to increase competition on the island mountain, which would leave less glory for them. Or in Augustine's words, they "begrudge others" a share of their vainglory, hoarding it for themselves, even as they generously point out the hidden rocks below to weary explorers seeking the land of bliss.[10]

Both of these geographic innovations are inspired by Augustine's embrace of Christianity. The Christian faith liberates Augustine from having to make Cicero's all-or-nothing argument about philosophy. If we have the assurances of a good God promising eternal life, it is not necessary that philosophy alone provide genuine happiness; it is not even necessary for us to attain happiness in this life in order to have a happy ending. Similarly, the unique Christian emphasis on the virtue of humility enables Augustine to see clearly the destructive effects of pride. The mountain dwellers never become truly happy because they are literally too elated by their own lofty positions to descend to the route that leads to the land of bliss. Humility, a virtue central to Christianity but not even mentioned in Aristotle's *Nicomachean Ethics*, keeps one from conflating the love of wisdom with the love of being loved for loving wisdom.

Three Classes of Sailors (1.2)

The maritime region that Augustine has charted serves as a backdrop to the three classes of seafarers who eventually reach the port of philosophy. The first consists of those who (1) have reached an "age fully possessed of reason," (2) arrive at the port with little effort, and (3) make or compose a work that serves as a beacon for others. Augustine does not stipulate at what age human beings come into full possession of their reason, but we may hazard a guess. In *On True Religion* (24.45), he describes boyhood, or *pueritia* (one to fourteen years old), as an age during which reason clings to "carnal or corporeal forms" by necessity; adolescence, or *adulescentia* (fifteen to thirty years old), as an age that clings to these material forms "almost necessarily"; and the ages afterwards (*juventus*, etc.) as periods during which this need increasingly fades. An age fully possessed of reason, then, is not the age at which children know when they are speaking the truth and when they are lying (sometime around the age of seven),[11] but the age at which it becomes less difficult for them to grasp incorporeal, intelligible reality. In the *Soliloquies*, Augustine expresses this grasp as having "eyes so healthy and vigorous that they can turn to the sun itself without any flinching as soon as they are opened" (1.13.23) — eyes that do not need to rely on lesser realities first. To be fully possessed of reason, then, is to be someone approximately thirty years old or older who fully understands the difference between the sensible and the intelligible.

Second, this first-class sailor is morally sound. Although no one is born a philosopher and therefore everyone to varying degrees starts out on the sea, these mariners are not far from the port. Not deceived by the enticing falsities of the open waters or inordinately attached to temporal goods, they prudently live moral and responsible lives. As a result, it is not difficult for them to reach port.

And third, these sailors raise, by virtue of a written work or composition, a bright "standard," or *signum*, for others to see—a literary lighthouse that beckons other ships safely home. Augustine does not stipulate who fits into this category, but one candidate would be Manlius Theodorus: at the time *On the Happy Life* was written, he was in his thirties, was a well-regarded Christian intellectual, and had composed books on philosophical subjects. But Augustine may also be thinking of his two adolescent students Licentius and Trygetius and his son Adeodatus, holding out the hope that they will, by the grace of God and with the help of these discussions, one day attain the fullest use of their reason without making the same mistakes that Augustine did as a young man.

The second class of sailors consists of those who have spent their lives obsessed with the goods of fortune all because a seemingly "favorable" tailwind led them into the delusion of taking these things seriously. Fortunately for them, however, a strong headwind in the form of personal tragedy now draws them to the books of the wise and the port of philosophy. (In this respect their lives recapitulate the shipwreck story of Zeno.) Here Augustine most likely has in mind his friends Romanianus, to whom he dedicates *Against the Academics*, and Zenobius, to whom he dedicates *On Order*. His goal is to lead both men, who were once successful or blessed in the eyes of the world but recently have been beset by misfortune, to the writings of the philosophers and to the love of wisdom through the agency of these dialogues.

Finally, the third class consists of those who fall somewhere in between—namely, they are not so privileged as the first class and not so desperate as the second. They are either at "the threshold of youth (*adulescentia*)," that is, not much older than fifteen, or have been tossed around for a few years on the open sea when they spot a *signum* (some wise book) that reminds them of their true homeland. They then either head home right away or are delayed by "clouds" and "sinking stars" until another calamity blows them in the right direction.

Although Augustine asks Theodorus to determine into which category he (Augustine) fits, it is fairly clear that he identifies most with the third. Augustine fell in love with philosophy at the age of eighteen while reading the *signum* of Cicero's *Hortensius* but was detained by the "cloudy" materialism of Manichaeism and the "sinking stars" of their superstitious astrology (1.4). The Academic skeptics helped rescue him from this debilitating dogmatism (despite his later criticisms of that school), and the "North Star" of Christianity has brought him close to the shore. Further, the writings of Plotinus, which he found to contain important truths that were compatible with orthodox Christian doctrine, greatly fanned his desire to come home. But it was not until an "adverse" tempest in the form of a chest pain compelled him to resign from his teaching position in rhetoric that he finally sailed into the port of philosophical leisure.

Lastly, as he is recounting his discovery of the North Star, Augustine makes a curious remark: "when one is thinking about God, one should in no way think about the body—nor when thinking about the soul*, since it is the one thing that is close to God" (1.4). It is a striking statement, one to which we will be compelled to return.

Added Layers

Two other aspects of Augustine's catalogue of sojourners merit our attention. First, each of the three classes makes some mention of books. The second class turns to books after being struck by tragedy, and the third class looks longingly at certain "standards" that point homeward. The first and very best class, on the other hand, does not need books but writes them for the benefit of others. Although he is predominantly from the third class, Augustine has something in common with all three. Like the first class, he is now composing books to serve as a beacon for others (he refers to *On the Happy Life* as so many *signa* in 1.5), and like the second, his sally into the port was caused by reading "the books of learned and very wise men" (1.2). Moreover, the prevalence of books highlights their importance in prompting the right kind of conversion to the good, and it highlights the potential value of Augustine's own dialogues.

Second, Augustine has infused this brief autobiography and the tales of the mariners with allusions to one of literature's most famous voyagers. The first class of sailors is reminiscent of Odysseus with the Phaeacians, whose island is not terribly far from Odysseus's home of Ithaca and whose ship is able to carry him there with little effort.[12] The hoisting of the "shining bright standard" could be in reference to the broad-bladed oar that Odysseus is supposed to plant in a land so far removed from the tumult of the sea that its inhabitants do not know what an oar is.[13] The second class of sailors, on the other hand, have become forgetful of home thanks to "favorable" winds that take them far away and who eventually return after "tearful" tragedies. These details roughly recall Odysseus's seven years on the island of Calypso, his longest sojourn after the Trojan War: the tearful tragedies suggest the depiction of Odysseus in the *Odyssey* weeping bitterly on the shores of Calypso's island.[14] Further, the third class remembers home and either heads out right away or is delayed by further enticements. In the first case, they are like Odysseus and the Lotus-Eaters, when Odysseus wastes no time in shoving off after he sees the amnesiac effect that lotus has on his crew.[15] In the second, they are like Odysseus with the goddess Circe, where he and his crew, forgetting their native land, are delayed for a year on her island by the carnal pleasures she provides.[16] Lastly, the call of the mountain-islanders that seduces travelers away from the port of philosophy echoes the song of the Sirens (1.2), those strange creatures whose enchanting music leads ships to their doom on the rocky coast of their island.[17] When, therefore, Augustine states that his profession of rhetoric was pointing him in the direction of the Sirens (1.4), he is implying that his career was tempting him onto the mountain of vainglory.

Augustine's references to Odysseus not only lend an epic and adventuresome quality to the journey of every soul that accepts the challenge to philosophize, but they constitute an artful development of a passage in the *Enneads*. After Plotinus expresses his approval of the advice in Homer's *Iliad*, "Let us flee to our beloved homeland," he relates this verse to the *Odyssey*. "For Odysseus," Plotinus explains, "is surely a parable to us when he commands the flight from the sorceries of Circe or Calypso—not content to linger for all the pleasure offered to his eyes and all the delight of sense filling his days."[18] Plotinus goes on to stipulate that the journey in question does not "bring us from land to land" but is an odyssey of the mind that involves "awakening" a kind of vision free of bodily eyes, a vision to which all have access but that few ever deign to attain.

Augustine's Present (1.5–6)

Augustine has come a long way in his own journey, but he is of the opinion that he still has a long way to go. Although he is now convinced that his happiness lies in joining the Catholic Church (for which he is currently preparing himself) and in the knowledge and love of the Triune God, he is still uncertain about exactly how to live his life accordingly. Moreover, he still has certain questions about the soul that trouble him.

Augustine therefore turns to Manlius Theodorus for spiritual direction. Theodorus is a respected member of the Christian Milanese circle of which Augustine is a part, and since Ambrose is too busy with his episcopal responsibilities,[19] it is natural for Augustine to turn to him. He later regrets the high praises he heaps on Theodorus,[20] but his flattery has a purpose: to persuade Theodorus to assess his (Augustine's) present condition and offer him guidance (1.4, 1.5). Indeed, Augustine is submitting *On the Happy Life* to him as the data from which Theodorus can draw up a full report.[21]

The Setting and Participants (1.6)

Augustine describes *On the Happy Life* as "more religious" (1.5) than his other dialogues, and it is easy to see why even apart from its explicit content. The setting of the baths is an unremarkable location for a philosophical dialogue, but the composition of the participants is unusual. It includes Augustine's brother Navigius, who is at least partially educated,[22] and his cousins Lartidianus and Rusticus, who are completely uneducated. Regarding the latter two, Augustine states that he wants to take advantage of their common sense, and he refers to their illiteracy gently, as their not having "endured" a single grammar school teacher. Despite the philosophical adage "Wisdom often dwells under a dirty cloak," and despite the fact that, according to Augustine, some writings make mention of philosopher-shoemakers,[23] lower-class figures nevertheless tend to be rare in philosophical dialogues. A slave boy has a minor role in Plato's *Meno* but not as a respected individual, and Cicero's dialogues are peopled with the elite of Republican Rome. Augustine recognizes the enormous difference between souls that are truly educated and souls that are not (see 2.8),[24] but in *On the Happy Life* he also evinces the desire that no one be left behind during these conversations (see 2.12, 2.16). His solicitude reflects the Christian conviction, evident in the fact of the Incarnation, that happiness and wisdom are not just for the few but for the many.[25]

Similarly remarkable is Augustine's inclusion of and praise for his uneducated mother Monica, who as a woman is greatly surprised to find herself in a philosophical dialogue.[26] Yet Augustine credits her with making him all that he is, and he refers to her not as "my mother" but "our mother," an epithet that extends beyond Augustine and Navigius to the entire group. Indeed, the example of Monica will serve as the main challenge to the opinion that one must be a philosopher in order to become happy or wise.

The time is also significant. *On the Happy Life* begins on November 13, 386, Augustine's thirty-second birthday. Augustine uses the occasion to host a banquet for the soul on the subject of happiness, a banquet that makes ample use of bodily metaphors concerning dining, tasting, and digestion. Both the occasion and the salience of this imagery stand in contrast to the philosopher Plotinus, who, it is reputed, never spoke of his ancestry or his birthplace and who refused to have a portrait of himself made because he seemed to be "ashamed of being in the body"[27] (in contrast to Cicero and Augustine, Plotinus also never went to the public baths).[28] As Augustine attests at 1.4, Plotinus's writings were greatly instrumental in his own philosophical progress, yet the content and literary conceit of *On the Happy Life* indicate a disagreement with Plotinus that points to a more positive view of the body and of the spatiotemporal world that, according to Christian belief, have both been created by an omnibenevolent God.

Lastly, the group has had a light lunch. Their moderation is the first sign of what will become a prominent theme in the dialogue, and it stands in contrast to the excesses characteristic of pagan feasts and the literature on them. But the moderate meal also ties in to Plato's *Symposium*, which likewise begins after a meal and likewise focuses on characters who are observing moderation as they discuss a single theme. Socrates's acquaintances in the *Symposium*, however, are moderate in their drinking because they are still hungover from the night before (176a–e). *On the Happy Life*, therefore, both stands within and departs from the philosophical literary tradition. It will be the reader's task to determine how and to what extent.

DAY ONE (2.7–16)
The Body-Soul Pairing (2.7–8)

Augustine begins by asking not whether the group *knows* that man consists of body and soul, but whether it *seems* obvious to them. He is not constructing an argument that would be invincible in the face of the most vigorous skepticism but one suited to a more commonsensical approach. The method and content of *On the Happy Life*, it is hinted, are different from that of its prequel *Against the Academics*.

In that same vein, Augustine is happy to circumvent technical terminology. When Navigius expresses doubt about the soul, Augustine moves dialectically from what Navigius knows (or thinks he knows) to the notion of the soul as the principle of life. Navigius is hesitant: he has probably read enough of Cicero to know that he needs to be careful about what he concedes. Proving that a man consists of body and soul, he rightly points out, does not prove that he consists only of body and soul.

But since Augustine is not seeking a definitive anthropology, he is content to have the group concede that a human being cannot exist without the body or the soul. (Interestingly, this means that a disembodied soul is no longer a human being, even if it remains a living and immortal human soul. Only the resurrection of the body at the end of time can restore the departed to their full humanity.) Augustine is also content to see the consumption of food linked to the body, even though he is aware that strictly speaking, physical hunger is also an activity or product of what some philosophers would call the appetitive part of the soul. He knows that the relationship between body and soul is too complicated to allow a strict dualism, but he tells the group that thinking in terms of these two is sufficient for what he wants (2.7)—namely, to direct their attention to the needs and aspirations of the highest part of the soul, a certain "divine something."[29]

Under Augustine's prompting, the group acknowledges that just as there is a food proper to the body, so too is there a food proper to the soul. Their assertion marks the first in a long series of analogies between the body and the soul, but it invites a cry of protest from the attentive reader, who a few pages earlier had read Augustine's declaration that, when thinking about the soul, one should *in no way* think about the body (1.4). How can such a statement be in the introduction to a three-day conversation that persistently compares the needs of the soul to those of the body? Is Augustine foolishly contradicting himself, or is his contradiction part of a greater design?

Only a careful analysis of the entire dialogue will yield a satisfactory answer, but at this point, we can make two observations. First, Augustine's working assumption in the dialogue proper, that the soul and the body are similar enough to each other to ground a litany of comparisons, may, in the final analysis, be more useful than true. In other words, Augustine's body-soul pairing may be like Socrates's equation of the city and the soul in Plato's *Republic,* an equation that holds enormous value in thinking through certain metaphysical and political topics but that breaks down in certain areas.

Second, the early part of the dialogue already reveals differences between the body and the soul. Both need nourishment, but as we will soon learn from Monica's example of Trygetius's behavior during lunch, the body and the soul are not always in agreement about what is to be nourished and when; in fact, they often tug in different directions. The dialogue begins after a deliberately light lunch because indulging the body can be detrimental to the soul's alacrity, with too much bodily consumption leading to too little mental activity. (Light dining, it turns out, is best for heavy thinking.) This tension between body and soul could be a testimony either to their similarity or to their difference.

Knowledge as Soul Food (2.8)

In answer to Augustine's question about whether knowledge is the soul's food, Monica, who lacks Navigius's hesitancy, asserts that the soul is fed by nothing else than the understanding and knowledge of things (2.8). Her answer is impressively philosophical, for it implies that wisdom, which the philosopher loves above all else, is the best food for the soul. One would have expected a more pious or explicitly religious answer from this devout matron. But Monica is willing to consider the human person on more natural terms, and she defends her view from Trygetius's doubts by making observations about his eating habits, when his mind was being nourished by one thing and his body by another. Monica's somewhat comical example shows her to be in a consistently maternal mode of concentration. Our first glimpse of her at Cassiciacum is interrupting the group's disputations and muscling them off to lunch (see *Against the Academics* 2.5.13), and here we see her solicitously monitoring the amount of food the young men have taken. We are beginning to see why Augustine refers to her as "our" mother.

But Monica's mundane example ties into a more serious point that is repeated elsewhere in the dialogues, namely, that human beings can be simultaneously occupied by different concerns and that when one of these concerns is bodily and the other intellectual, it is a possible indication of a certain freedom of the intellectual from the bodily—or at least a difference between the two.[30] The mind's "getting lost in thought" means that there *is* a mind to get lost, a reality that cannot be explained entirely in terms of the body's various functions, not even the brain's. As Licentius asks in *Against the Academics:* "What does it mean that we hunger more persistently for one thing when our mind is intent on something else? Or what is it that becomes so exceedingly domineering when we are occupied with our hands and teeth?" (2.4.10).

The *je-ne-sais-quoi* "divine something" to which Licentius and Monica are drawing the listeners' attention is similar to the Cartesian *res cogitans* or "thinking thing" but with at least one crucial difference. Monica's starting point is not with thinking but with knowing, which is why she adds that in order for the mind to be nourished, it must be fed on thoughts and theories through which something can be perceived; she is interested in mental activities that connect to reality. Knowing involves thinking, but it is more than that: I can think of unicorns all day, but it does not necessarily bring me closer to a knowledge of the real. Thoughts and theories disconnected from reality are like an infant sucking its own thumb instead of its mother's breast.

Monica's statement triggers the greatest amount of disagreement in the entire three days of discussion. Based on the conversation of the first book of *Against the Academics,* which has already taken place,[31] we can imagine that the quarrel is partially caused by Licentius, the self-declared skeptic who would prefer to think of the mind being nourished by the *search* for wisdom instead of its actual attainment. He would, in turn, be challenged by Trygetius, the self-declared nemesis of the skeptics. But what about the rest of the group? Perhaps there is a latent materialism in their thinking that has difficulty conceiving of thoughts and theories, even when they are of the real, as providing genuine sustenance.

Augustine therefore approaches the same conclusion from a different perspective. Are not the minds of the genuinely educated, he asks, "fuller" than those of the uneducated? It is a delicate question, considering that most in the group are uneducated. Their sudden and ready acquiescence is puzzling. Are they intimidated? Are they hiding hurt feelings? Or are they simply rising above their own personal lives to judge the matter impartially? If the latter, then they are exhibiting a certain "fullness" of judgment despite being unlearned—an act that is perhaps not enough to refute the statement they have affirmed but enough to qualify it. And what are we to make of Augustine's ostensible discourtesy and insensitivity, with his talk about the unlearned being barren, hungry, and mangy, all in front of his unlearned relatives? Augustine's harsh words must be seen in juxtaposition to his portrayal of his mother Monica, who, although at best partially educated in the liberal arts, is not intellectually diseased or mangy.

Finally, it should be noted that the terminology has been quietly changed. Initially, Augustine's question was about the soul (*anima*) and the nourishment proper to it. Monica also speaks of *anima*, but midway through her response to Trygetius, she uses *animus* (translated in these passages as "mind"), and for the rest of the paragraph the discussion revolves around the notion of *animus*. (When Augustine returns to the language of *anima* in 2.9, it is clear that he has in mind human *animae*.) Monica's shift in diction is understandable since she is drawing attention to the part of Trygetius's soul that is engaged in mental concentration: and whereas *anima* is the term for a soul that inhabits any living thing, *animus* is the term for a rational and therefore uniquely human soul.[32] But the change is also providential, for it eliminates a previous weakness in Augustine's opening statement on the subject. Initially, Augustine had claimed that "knowledge" (*scientia*) is the food of the soul (*anima*), and yet animals, which possess an *anima*, cannot possess the highest form of knowledge known as *scientia*.[33] The group, however, never detects the weakness in the initial formulation, suggesting that it is not "full" of the highest level of philosophical acumen.

Frugality as Fullness (2.8)

Trygetius's blunt remark about the unlearned, that their minds "are full of defects and worthlessness" (2.8), prompts Augustine to offer an explanation that he does not expect everyone to understand. Fullness in reference to the defective, he states, is actually a form of emptiness. Souls not filled with knowledge or virtue are "filled with" an empty and unnourishing junk food. Augustine will return to this surprisingly difficult topic later on (see 4.29).

It is also in this section that Augustine, borrowing some clever etymologies from Cicero, juxtaposes nothingness and the vice of worthlessness (*nequitia*) with fruitfulness and the virtue of frugality. His association of fullness with frugality runs counter to our own assumptions of frugality as a kind of stinginess, assumptions that would place frugality more in the category of emptiness than of fullness. To be sure, the Latin *frugalitas* was used as the equivalent of the Greek *sōphrosunē*, or "healthy-mindedness," a word that denotes a well-balanced and virtuous life. Nevertheless, even *sōphrosunē* connotes an element of thrift or economy, of holding back for the sake of balance and virtue. How, then, can frugality be a form of fullness?

Augustine's answer lies in his explanation that frugality receives its name from the "fruitfulness of the mind" that it confers. To put it in a more modern idiom, self-restraint is paradoxically essential for personal fulfillment. Even on a purely hedonistic level, maximizing one's carnal pleasures requires moderation, since it does not take long for an excess of pleasure—as can be seen, for instance, in the consumption of alcohol—to become unpleasant. Subsequently, even the pleasure-seeking Epicureans promoted the virtue of moderation. And if moderation is essential for the pleasures of the body, it is especially essential for the thriving of the mind or soul. As we saw in the case of the "light lunch," exercising due restraint in bodily delights paves the way for heightened satisfaction in intellectual activities; it is a holding back in a lesser area in order to yield a greater abundance in another. And as we learn in 2.13, this holding back or modulating of one's desires and activities is also important in purely intellectual pursuits, even in the pursuit of truth itself. Moderation, we see again, is crucial.

The Banquet of Bliss (2.9–10)

After succeeding in his quest to have the group concede that there is a food proper to the soul (and that the soul is different from the body), Augustine feels that he "ought to provide" a banquet of soul food on the occasion of his birthday. In using the language of duty (the verb *debere* he uses for "ought" implies moral necessity), Augustine playfully assumes the position of an important patron throwing a birthday party for his dependents and clients. There is nothing unusual in this arrangement (such parties were standard in the intricate Roman world of patronage),[34] aside from the obvious fact that Augustine is not a patron in the conventional sense of that term. And there is another curious detail: Augustine speaks of preparing the meal himself, as if he were a chef (2.9). Even when a chef's work was highly prized (and it often was), the position itself was held in low regard by the Romans: cooks, for instance, were excluded from military service because they were involved in a "degraded profession." Augustine, the leader and guest of honor, is therefore taking on a subservient and even humiliating role. This twist to the proposal has an echo of Plato's *Symposium*, when Agathon, the host of the evening, tells his servants to act as if the diners were *their* guests and to choose the dishes accordingly (175b). There is a hint of the inverted or topsy-turvy in Augustine's playful conceit.

Augustine's cerebral dinner proposal is not novel. Socrates speaks of the dialogue that transpires in Plato's *Timaeus* as a "feast of words" (20c), and the *Symposium*'s various speeches in praise of Eros are meant to replace a postprandial bout of heavy drinking (177e). In Macrobius's *Saturnalia*, the character Eustathius defends the invitation of Lady Philosophy to their banquet (7.1). Feasting and philosophizing, or philosophizing as a form of feasting, go hand in hand.

Augustine's proposal also explains why the conversation has taken the somewhat circuitous path that it has. He stresses the need for his guests to have an appetite for what he is to feed them, and his very explanation seems designed to whet that appetite. From the beginning, Augustine has been piquing the group's interest through a method of tantalization, dangling intriguing ideas in a roundabout way but holding back on his full intentions. The hunger he is trying to awaken through this method is crucial, for without it, there can be no genuine knowledge or wisdom. Human knowledge comes to an individual only as the result of

personal curiosity or desire. It must be born of inquiry and cona-
tion; otherwise, what one holds to be true is merely opinion or
unverified belief. And there is an additional benefit to this method.
By awakening the group's intellectual hunger, or *eros*, and thema-
tizing it, Augustine is making them more cognizant of it, and by
making them more cognizant of it, he is helping them see for
themselves that there is a native *eros* or drive unique to the human
intellect, one that has its own special needs different from those
of the body.

Of course, although everyone, by virtue of being born a rational
animal, has this native *eros*, not everyone is immediately capable of
fanning and satiating it. Augustine points out that only healthy minds
yearn for spiritual food, while "sick" minds spit it out. This sickness
may come from being uneducated, which leaves one, as we have
already been told, diseased and mangy. Education is about not only
learning something true, but cultivating the right desire for learning.
Without that cultivation, the soul is likely to resist the very thing that
will make it well.

The feast that Augustine has prepared is on the nature of happiness (2.10). Happiness is a subject in which all—young and old,
educated and uneducated—are interested, for all human beings
yearn to be happy. The group arrives quickly at two conclusions:
there is a desire for happiness, and happiness consists in the fulfillment of desire (if someone has an unfulfilled desire, he or she
cannot be happy). But further qualifications are necessary. First,
happiness does not come from the fulfillment of bad desires: heroin
addicts may be able to satiate their cravings, but no one would call
junkies happy. Happiness, then, requires not only fulfillment or
possession, but the cultivation of good desires and the extirpation
of bad ones, a fact that again invites us to a consideration of *eros*.
(There is a second qualification as well that comes later.)

Augustine praises Monica for immediately seeing the importance of right *eros* and praises her for having mastered "the very
citadel of philosophy." As Augustine's praise would indicate, Monica's
second contribution to the conversation (see 2.8 for her first) is a
good one. But does capturing philosophy's stronghold ipso facto
make someone a philosopher?

Monica utters a zesty exclamation at Augustine's recitation of
Cicero's words from the *Hortensius,* leading the group to forget for a
moment that she is a woman. Especially to modern readers, this reaction seems to be an instance of male chauvinism, but the wording
suggests a somewhat different explanation. Augustine stipulates that
his mother exclaimed in such a way that they all thought they were
in the presence of a *great* man, the emphasis being on the adjective
rather than the noun. Philosophy may be difficult for women, but it
is difficult for men, too, which is why only the truly exceptional, male
or female, make true philosophers. And while it is no doubt the case
that when the group thinks of a great philosopher, they think of a
great man (since all the great philosophers of the classical period
were male), Augustine elsewhere explicitly affirms that women can
also be philosophers (see *On Order* 1.11.31). Further, the clause about
"thoroughly forgetting her sex" ties into the classical teaching that
sexual differentiation pertains to the body rather than the soul.
Unlike their bodies, the souls of men and women are not only equal,
but identical. By "forgetting her sex," then, Augustine is saying that
Monica was behaving in such a manner that the group was impressed
by the greatness of her soul. It is a high compliment during a discussion on the soul.

Augustine's praise of Monica is quickly followed by a chas-
tisement of Licentius. Augustine describes the youth's suggestion
as "modest and deferential," essentially admitting that there was
nothing inappropriate or unreasonable in his request to stipulate

the desires that are conducive to happiness. Indeed, Augustine obliges the request a moment later. Why, then, does he speak abruptly to Licentius in a way that shames him into silence? The answer may have something to do with the mounting tension between the two characters. Licentius's earlier contribution to the discussion was needling. At 2.7, he objected to Augustine's contention that all bodies have a limit fixed on them by nature which will suffer when afflicted by malnourishment on the grounds that growing lean is not the same as growing less. While the statement is true as far as it goes, it is persnickety in context. Now he is telling Augustine what to do before he has had a chance to do it, which is not only impertinent, but annoying, especially if the requested item was already intended to be introduced later as something of a surprise. Perhaps Augustine is looking at Licentius as one of those students who disrupts class with bursts of insistent enthusiasm but never puts in the effort to do the homework or follow the instructor's carefully prepared course of study. Certainly, later interactions between Augustine and Licentius will witness a teacher's frustration with his pupil.[35]

The Nature of Happiness (2.11)

Augustine's next step is to establish that if someone is not happy, he or she is miserable. The group has "no doubts" that this is so, but the contemporary reader is liable to react much differently. Part of the problem is cultural and linguistic. In English, we do not hesitate to speak of degrees of happiness, and we associate misery (*miseria*) only with a state of total abjection or destitution. We therefore tend to think of supreme happiness and utter misery as the opposite ends of a spectrum with a multitude of possibilities in between.

But Augustine will grant no such middle ground any more than he will grant a middle ground between being alive and dead (see 4.24). His "extremism" has three causes. First, he is following the Platonic predilection for the unqualified noun as the designation of a perfected object, or to put it differently, the contention that a thing is really a thing only when that thing is at its very best. That Augustine uses this method is evident later on, when he equates being a "great man" to being a "real man" (2.16). But if only a great man is a real man, then there is a way in which a mediocre man is not really a man at all. In the words of Ernest Fortin: "As its etymology implies, the term 'perfection,' from the Latin *perficere*, 'to bring to completion,' is synonymous with wholeness"; and to the extent to which a property that belongs to a thing is lacking, that thing "is less than what its name indicates."[36] Augustine's strategy, which he employs throughout his life to great rhetorical effect, is to study things "in light of their highest metaphysical principles."[37] And in light of such principles, it makes as much sense to claim that you are somewhat happy as it does to say that you are partially pregnant.

Second, throughout the Cassiciacum dialogues Augustine is responding to Cicero, who likewise takes a rigorous Platonic line on the exclusivity of happiness and misery. For Cicero, speaking of degrees of misery is like distinguishing between a man who is drowning one inch below the surface of the water and a man who is drowning at the bottom of the sea:

> For as those who have been submerged under water cannot breathe—even if they are not very far from the surface (though they may on this account be able to emerge now and then)—any more than if they were at the bottom; nor can the puppy who is now on the verge of seeing see any more than the puppy who was

just born: so too, the man who has made some progress toward the possession of virtue is no less in a state of misery than the one who has made no progress at all.[38]

Part of Augustine's strategy in the Cassiciacum dialogues is to beat Cicero at his own game, so to speak, accepting his parameters and showing that the incredibly high standards set by the Platonic-Ciceronian tradition can be fulfilled only by the Christian faith.

Third, Augustine is not interested in lessening the pain and despair of our frail and mortal existence so that we can muster just enough strength to get out of bed in the morning and greet another day, nor he is interested in spiritual narcotics that alleviate the symptoms but leave the disease untouched. Augustine wants to identify and *reach* supreme happiness and bliss, and as such he is seeking the source of total human fulfillment. The value in Augustine's approach, even for those not sharing its presuppositions, is that in forcing us to consider what ultimate human happiness would consist of, it forces us to discover our human nature—that which is to be fulfilled or perfected.

Augustine is now in a position to satisfy Licentius's request and examine the question "what should a man acquire for himself in order to be happy?" (2.11). If happiness is to be supreme and abiding, it cannot involve anything dependent on fortune or accident, since such goods can just as easily be taken away as they can be given. Earlier, Augustine had said that "something *is* if it remains, if it stays constant, if it is always the same" (2.8); here, he adds that if we want to be permanently happy, we need a good that is of such a caliber.

Trygetius objects. What if we have goods that can be potentially taken away but in fact are not being taken away? What about all the wealthy individuals who have amassed goods vulnerable to fortune and yet nevertheless live without misfortune? Augustine responds that such individuals still live in fear that their goods can be taken away from them. Indeed, the more goods you have, the more you have to fear over their potential loss.

Monica adds that if a wealthy man *is* happy, he is happy by virtue of the moderation of his mind, not by virtue of what he owns. Pursuit of the American dream, for instance, has led some to fame and fortune, but when these industrious go-getters do not possess moral virtue, their affluence becomes the occasion not of happiness, but of misery and even self-destruction—they are, to borrow a phrase from Tocqueville, beset by a strange melancholy in the midst of plenty.[39] By privileging the goods of the soul (the virtue of moderation) over those of the body (money), Monica is for a second time qualifying the earlier statement that happiness consists in the fulfillment of desire. Before, it was conceded that only good desires must be fulfilled (2.10); now it is conceded that only the very best desires need to be fulfilled; and the desire for bodily goods, because of those goods' intrinsic instability, is not among them.

What can fulfill those desires, the group concludes, is God. Both Trygetius and Licentius, however, are eager to move on. Trygetius says, "We agreed to this a little while ago" (2.11)—as if to say, "Hurry up!"—while Licentius says that God's eternal nature is so self-evident that there is no need for further inquiry. Ever since the conversation has turned to the subject of happiness, the group has been quickly assenting to almost every point that Augustine has made—unlike before, when they greeted almost every question with an objection or further discussion. Such haste may be explained by the group's eagerness to learn the secret of happiness; they are willing to agree to almost anything if it means that Augustine will cut to the chase and reveal it. Compounding this eagerness is the fact that none of them is trained in logic or dialectic (which instills a greater sense of caution), and even if they were, it would not guarantee the required self-discipline. Augustine is a master dialectician, yet he commits the same mistake of haste in the *Soliloquies* that the group is committing here, despite Reason's explicit warnings.[40]

Augustine's argument, which concludes with the proposition that he who has God is happy, is missing several planks. If happiness is the possession of something eternal and abiding, could not the possession of geometric truths confer happiness, since they too are eternal and abiding?[41] And yet it seems fairly obvious that becoming a geometer does not necessarily make one happy. A conversation that took place a few days earlier, however, fills in some of the gaps. In book one of *Against the Academics*, after the group has asserted that all people want to be happy, Augustine states that "living happily" is "living according to that which is best in man," with the "best" defined as mind or reason, "that ruling part of the soul which the other parts in man should obey."[42] But if mind or reason is fulfilled only when it has grasped all truth, mind or reason will be satisfied only by a grasp of total intelligibility. And in the Christian tradition God is this total intelligibility, the most meaningful of all possible "objects" of thought and the source of all other meaning even though God is an "object" or source like no other. In other parts of the Cassiciacum dialogues Augustine will speak of God as man's *summum bonum*, or supreme good,[43] and as he explains elsewhere outside of the Cassiciacum corpus, although the supreme good is not necessarily the only good, it is the one good to which all others are related:

> For someone is happy when he enjoys that for the sake of which he wants everything else, since it is now being loved, not for the sake of something else, but for its own sake. And so, the goal is

said to be there because at this point nothing is found toward which it can go forth or to which it is related. There one finds the desire's rest, there the assurance of enjoyment, there the most tranquil joy of a perfect will.[44]

Augustine may have omitted these considerations because the group has agreed, not through a process of philosophical ratiocination, but through "pious devotion" (2.11). The group believes that God is eternal and abiding by virtue of their faith, whereas Augustine had arrived at that conclusion through his study of the Platonists before he became a believer.[45] Similarly, the group has no difficulty in identifying God as the source of their happiness.

Got God? Preliminary Definitions (2.12)

It now remains for the group to determine what it means to "have God." The very phrase strikes the modern reader as odd, perhaps even selfish or possessive. Yet it must be remembered that like wisdom, God is perfectly shareable, and there is never anything selfish in the pejorative sense about pursuing or attaining the perfectly shareable, even when it is done for the sake of fulfilling oneself.[46] In the *Soliloquies* Augustine succinctly defines having God as seeing God (1.1.3), hardly a "possessive" act. Moreover, the equation of "having God" with happiness echoes the etymological meaning of happiness in Greek, since *eudaimonia* literally means to have a good god or *daimon* in you.

Augustine wants to hear his interlocutors' thoughts on having God, not because he is uncertain himself (see *Soliloquies* 1.1.3), but because he again wants to excite the intellectual *eros* of the group by exercising their minds. And the group's various definitions reveal something about the state of each of the characters' intellectual *eros*.

Licentius, the assertive pupil who is usually the first to speak, defines having God as "living well." He offers the most philosophical of the definitions: it reflects Aristotle's definition of happiness as living well, and it conforms with the important notion that happiness is an activity rather than a good feeling.[47] But it is also the least determinate and, possibly, the most prone to misappropriation. Even a pleasure-fixated Epicurean might agree with this statement, and so might an Academic skeptic. No one else joins Licentius in this opinion.

Trygetius defines having God as doing "what God wants done." Doing the will of God is, of course, essential to Christianity, but Trygetius's wording *may* suggest a voluntaristic focus on blind obedience. An army veteran, Trygetius is construing happiness in terms of promptly carrying out the orders of the cosmos' supreme commander. Augustine's illiterate cousins Lartidianus and Rusticus agree with Trygetius, implicating this definition as possibly the least sophisticated.

Adeodatus defines having God as not having "an unclean spirit": instead of Trygetius's external emphasis on right response, Adeodatus focuses on something more fundamental, internal purity. His definition, which reflects his own impressive purity,[48] is the most explicitly theological answer of them all, the one most dependent on Church parlance, which is why Augustine will have to consult ecclesiastical usage in order to parse out its meaning. The definition's only peculiarity is its use of a double negative. Why does Adeodatus say that having God is not having an unclean spirit rather than having a clean spirit? Whatever the reasoning behind his wording, pious Monica and Navigius agree with the definition.

Augustine again makes certain that no one is left out of the discussion, drawing in Navigius and the bashful Rusticus. Augustine is not simply being a hospitable host (which in itself is an important mark of one's graciousness, or *humanitas*) but a Christian one. We shall revisit this point later.

Augustine's Birthday Cake and Licentius's Reaction (2.13–15)

Augustine pauses here in the name of moderation, again demonstrating the importance of measure (2.13). Just as there can be a deficiency in nourishment for both body and soul that leads to starvation, so too can there be an excess that leads to physical and mental indigestion. Augustine literally says that excessive food makes one "digest poorly," that it induces an inability to break down and appropriate what one has received. Teachers must keep their students somewhat hungry all the time and never overwhelm them, for students will not only fail to learn but begin to resent the learning process. Arousing intellectual *eros* is a crucial component of education. Augustine's odd phrasing, "this question will treat us better tomorrow when we are hungry" (2.13), suggests that it is not we who take up the question but the question that takes up us, even if we do not consciously know the destination. And the question is practically meaningless without the hunger, or *eros*; indeed, it is impossible to separate the two.

Augustine will leave the group with a small consolation treat, one that actually excites rather than satiates their eagerness — which, of course, was his intention all along. He offers this treat on the grounds that it is customary to end a banquet with dessert (2.13). Augustine is right to assert that honey nut cakes, a metaphorical version of which he is serving now, were not uncommon as the final course of a Roman banquet. But what is odd is that the group has not reached the end of the banquet but its intermission, since they will resume on the same point tomorrow. Corporeal and intellectual feasts have much in common, but they also differ. Not surprisingly, Augustine does not designate this treat with a specific noun but speaks of "things of this sort" (2.13). The Romans offered a cake called a *libum* or a *placenta* on their birthdays to their *genius* (roughly, a personal god or spirit), but Augustine avoids these terms, presumably because of their pagan connotations.

Like the question that takes up the group, Augustine says that the idea has come to him suddenly, a testimony to the adventitious or giftlike quality of his insight. He presents this gift to the group as a "waiter" and "server" (2.13). Before, Augustine was the chef; now, he assumes an even humbler position. The topsy-turvy element of this banquet, with Augustine acting as a servant rather than a leader (or better, a servant-leader) continues. When Augustine the waiter brings out the tray from the kitchen of his mind, the group "rises up" to help him with outstretched hands: literally, the text states, "they made themselves erect." The language of standing upright or becoming erect is significant, as it implies reason's coming into its own, a rising up to a higher, more intelligent, viewpoint.[49] The group's intellectual desire, aroused by Augustine's enticement, has energized or awakened their reason.

The dessert consists of a rebuff of the Academic skeptics, who were the subject of a conversation a few days earlier involving Augustine, Licentius, Trygetius, and Navigius.[50] Trygetius has been a critic of the Academic position (which explains his unbridled glee over the disparaging dessert) and Licentius a defendant (which explains his displeasure and frustration). Licentius is also holding out for Alypius, who was absent from that debate and who will later take the Academic side (2.14).[51] Licentius cannot expose a flaw in the argument but spiritedly rejects it nonetheless. He calls the treat a lure or a trap and refuses to acknowledge it as a syllogistic argument, referring to it instead somewhat contemptuously as a "little whatever-it-is," or *hoc nescio quid breve* (2.15). He even attempts to manipulate the stenographers' recording of the conversation by denying something he said that he knew would not redound to his credit (2.15). Having invested his ego into a defense of the Academics, Licentius is concerned not so much about the truth, but about being right or at least appearing to be right in the eyes of others.

Narrating the behavior that results from this investment of the ego, Augustine writes that Licentius laughs "testily"—the word used is *stomachanter,* an adverb pertaining to the digestive system (2.15). Licentius's testiness epitomizes the conflict between the love of wisdom and the love of reputation, or put differently, between the desire to see what is real versus the desire to be seen unrealistically. Threatened with a publicizing of his intellectual deficiencies by having them written down, Licentius fears losing face in front of others. We will see in *On Order* what happens when the desire for a good reputation remains uncorrected. Here, Augustine endeavors to use this vanity against itself as a goad to be reasonable. Are you sure you want to go on record, Augustine prods him, with the asinine position that the man who does not have what he wants is totally happy? (2.15). What will others think? In order to be perceived as intelligent, is it not the best policy to *be* intelligent? But being intelligent means pursuing the truth outside oneself rather than cultivating appearances about oneself. Augustine endeavors to use Licentius's concern for self-image as a means of moving him beyond it, channeling his ego-ridden "shame," with its constant yet changing posturing, toward a more thoughtful "consistency."

A Bittersweet Dessert and Navigius's Reaction (2.13–15)

The reaction of Navigius, who has no invested interest in the debate about the Academics and who must be teased into the discussion, is more intriguing (2.14). Speaking ambivalently, Augustine warns of the effects of sweets on his brother's spleen, a comment that could refer to a preexisting health condition or possibly to Navigius's being "splenetic" metaphorically, that is, ill-humored or irritable. Augustine's language is loaded in another way as well: the phrase he uses for a bad spleen, *splen vitiosus*, is taken from Columella's description of pigs, whose excessive (*supra modum*) love of sweetness in their food causes an inflammation of the spleen that can be cured by water infused with bitter tamarisk.[52] The theme of moderation again emerges in the dialogue, albeit implicitly.

Navigius laughs good-naturedly at the fraternal jibe, demonstrating that at least he is not splenetic metaphorically (2.14). He acknowledges the logic of his brother's argument as sound, citing its curative properties. (Honey was a common ingredient in medicinal potions.) But Navigius also calls Augustine's honey bittersweet as well as tangled and prickly. Technically, his remarks are complimentary, meant to show that Augustine's concoction is tart enough to cure an inflamed spleen.[53] But the compliment is left-handed and wryly contains the same mixture of sweetness and bitterness as its object: the phrase Navigius employs, "tangled as well as prickly," was originally coined by Cicero in reference to sophisms. Even if he cannot put his finger on it, Navigius senses that there is something not quite right about Augustine's birthday cake, that somewhere in it is a dollop of sophistry. Finally, it is noteworthy that Navigius, apparently aware of the allusion to Columella, has borrowed lines from Cicero in order to fashion a response. Navigius may not have his brother's level of erudition, but he is not completely uneducated either.

Augustine's birthday cake is initially laid out in nine indicative statements (2.14), but he reduces them to three for Licentius:

(1) someone who does not have what he wants is unhappy, (2) the Academics want to discover the truth, and (3) he who is not happy is not wise (2.15). The first proposition logically follows from what has already been conceded, and the second is a favorable assessment of the Academics' quest for wisdom, which neither Augustine nor Licentius would deny. Only the third proposition is new to the group, but it is common in Ciceronian and Stoic thought. Although Licentius is far from a perfect disciple of Cicero, he would be loath to contradict Cicero knowingly, on whose authority he relied heavily during the conversation in book one of *Against the Academics*.

Augustine compares his three propositions to three ingredients —honey, flour, and nuts—but he does not say whether each proposition is to align with a particular ingredient (2.15). Perhaps the metaphor should be construed more broadly, with the dessert in its entirety containing all of what the three ingredients symbolize. Flour or ground meal (*far*) was a hardy source of nutrition for the Romans, while nuts—or more specifically, the kernel of nuts (*nuclei*)—may signify the heart of the matter. But it is the honey that occupies most of the conversation. At first, Augustine mentions only this ingredient, when he refers to it as "scholastic" (2.13). Navigius adds that it is Hymettic, a wild honey found near Athens, the birthplace of philosophy. The bittersweetness of Augustine's complex honey, we may conjecture, tastes like Socratic irony or dissemblance.

But what is it that Navigius detects to be amiss? It may be the fact that the birthday cake topples not only the Academics, but everyone else as well, including Augustine and those like him who seek wisdom but cannot claim to have found it. Although Augustine's prickly and tangled "lure" serves the intended function of dethroning the Academics as distinguished authorities, it also exposes the fact that everyone else is also unhappy and unwise.[54] This is a bitter truth, one that is perhaps best revealed only when accompanied by a "sweet truth" to balance it out (whether Augustine will do so remains to be seen). In any case, beneath this playful attack on the Academics is the more serious point that skepticism, despite its claims to the contrary, falls short of authentic human happiness. Happiness is fulfillment, while searching necessarily implies a lack that stands in need of being filled. This conviction, which constitutes the "kernel" of Augustine's phenomenology of happiness, points to the source of humanity's ultimate "nourishment" in God.

Monica's Slur (2.16)

Augustine, noticing that not everyone is laughing and that some are put off by the ravenous behavior of the others, is disturbed by the inequality at the table. The host of this verbal banquet is not an egalitarian in the sense that he equates all forms of inequality with injustice, but he recognizes that all friendship, even friendship between unequal parties, tends in the direction of equality.[55] And although it is not stated explicitly, Augustine is inspired by Manlius Theodorus's *Christian* example of inviting everyone to the feast. Natural and conventional inequalities in humankind notwithstanding, Christianity is for the many as well as for the few, binding all into one shareable and mystical body.

Further, Christian teaching links greatness to humility. To be a great man, a real man, Augustine must become a lowly man, thus continuing the topsy-turvy element of his banquet and readily heeding Christ's admonition: "whosoever will be the greater among you, let him be your minister, and he that will be first among you, shall be your servant, even as the Son of man is not come to be ministered unto but to minister" (Matt 20:26–28). Augustine therefore takes on yet another servile role, that of a summoner, or *invitator*, a Roman slave who goes out and invites guests to his master's feast. He turns to his mother as a servant to his mistress. Monica, readily responding as the lady of a great manor, "was only too glad to command that what they had less of should be brought forth as if it were from her very own cellar" (2.16). Augustine, in turn, refrains from doing something until his mother explicitly bids it. This exchange between a son/servant and a mother about a wine cellar thus has faint overtones of the wedding at Cana (see John 2:1–12), with Monica as a figure of the Virgin Mary, who instructs both her son and the servants about procuring more wine even though it is not her cellar, so to speak.

Monica issues a command to the *invitator*, ordering Augustine to provide an account of the Academics. After he does so, the great mistress of the manor, who apparently also has little patience for the endless ratiocinations of skepticism, pronounces judgment: the Academics are epileptics, or "spazzes." No English word can quite capture all of the aspects of Monica's humorous and politically incorrect putdown. The word *caducarius* is colloquial or "lowbrow" (*vulgaris*), as her son Navigius later puts it (3.20), and most likely it is North African in origin, which would explain why Augustine feels compelled to explain its meaning to the Milanese recipient of the dialogue, Manlius Theodorus. The slur does, however, convey her critique with great accuracy: just as epileptics are not in control of their bodies during an epileptic fit, Academics are mentally out of control when they consistently refuse to assent to the truth. The result is identical in both cases: they fall instead of rise, the opposite of "becoming erect" (see above).

Caducarius can also relate to property that does not fall to its rightful heir. Seen from this additional perspective, the Academics are those who are bereft of a true legacy. After changing his mind about the Academics, Licentius elsewhere calls them captious, as if they were legacy hunters who rob others of their inheritance.[56]

Lastly, Monica's epithet hearkens to a passage in Plato's *Lesser Hippias* where Socrates, apologizing for the confusion he has caused his interlocutor Hippias, refers to his vacillations of opinion as a kind of *katabolē* (372e). Because this Greek word for a periodic fit of illness literally refers to a throwing or falling down (not unlike the Latin *caducarius*), one translator has rendered it as "seizure."[57] By this reckoning, Socrates (who appears to most of Athens as ever-bumbling) is calling himself an intellectual epileptic. But if Socrates, the paragon of the philosophical life, is an epileptic, is being an epileptic or chronic waffler constitutive of being a philosopher? If so, Monica is most gladly denying that she is or ever will be a philosopher.

DAY TWO (3.17–22)
Got God? Further Considerations (3.17–18)

The next day, the same people take the same seats in the same location, but they begin a "little later" than when they last left off (3.17). The identical positions of the interlocutors suggest a continuation of what was initiated the day before, while the relatively late start explains why today's conversation is not as long as that of the previous day. Augustine also continues the banquet motif, making self-deprecating jokes about leftovers and meager fare.

But there is a shift as well. When Augustine first proposed his feast of words, he spoke of things that he had prepared for his guests (2.9). Now, he denies not only preparing the food, but even knowing what dishes have been prepared. Someone else, a divine host or chef, is providing these exquisite courses. Augustine portrays himself as a passive agent in this and in other ways. Yesterday, Augustine himself had asked the group whom they thought "had" God (2.12); now, he uses the passive voice—"it was asked" who had

God—in order to hint that reason, not he, is guiding the discussion. Indeed, according to Augustine it is reason rather than faith that has proved that someone who has God is happy (3.17), even though the group had agreed "with pious devotion" (2.11). God and reason, it is implied, are not incompatible; in this passage, they function almost interchangeably. Augustine expresses confidence in both and in the belief that there is a benevolent, providential order guiding this rational discussion.

Augustine next reconciles the group's various definitions of having God. He repeats their positions, although he changes the order by putting Trygetius's definition before Licentius's, and he charitably speaks of "some" (in the plural) who said that having God is living well in order to brush over the potentially embarrassing fact that no one else sided with Licentius. Augustine has little difficulty demonstrating the compatibility of the first two definitions, the order of which he changes again, as if to underscore their synonymy, for "living well is nothing else but doing the things that please God" (3.18). Deciphering Adeodatus's double-negative definition, on the other hand, requires more effort. To aid him, Augustine draws from ecclesiastical usage and the liturgy of the Church, which, like Scripture, is an authoritative part of the divine mysteries in which he as a catechumen is eager to participate. According to the sacred liturgy, an unclean spirit can be either a demon that possesses human beings and requires an exorcist to be removed or a human soul sullied by vice and error. The last condition is significant: Augustine does not limit "uncleanness" to moral impurity but extends it to the intellectual failing of error.[58]

Augustine does not know which meaning of an unclean spirit his son has in mind, and so he asks him to clarify. In this, the longest exchange between Augustine and Adeodatus in the Cassiciacum dialogues, the boy explains that he means not merely an absence of demonic possession, but a life lived "chastely," which he construes as paying attention to God and being devoted to Him alone (3.18). Adeodatus has a robust understanding of chastity that goes beyond the mere absence of illicit sexual activity to a life centered positively on God. That Augustine has Adeodatus's words written down verbatim indicates the extent to which he is impressed with his son's reply. Given Adeodatus's clarification, it is not difficult to reconcile his definition with the other notions of living well and obeying God.

The Creeping Syllogism (3.19)

Having consolidated their opinions, Augustine now moves to a new series of propositions: (1) God wants humans to seek God, (2) the person who seeks God lives well, and (3) an unclean spirit cannot seek God. Navigius hesitates at the third but eventually yields to peer pressure and agrees with the others.

Augustine then offers a new argument that can be reformulated thus. God wants us to seek Him; therefore, someone who seeks God is doing what God wants. If we are doing what God wants, we are also living well and free of any unclean spirit (as conceded earlier). But seeking God means *not having* God. Yet was it not concluded that living well and not having an unclean spirit and doing what God wants all mean that we "have" God, that we are no longer seeking Him?

Augustine has offered what may be called a "creeping syllogism," a term inspired by his description of arguments that creep along little by little into a false conclusion (see *On Order* 2.5.14). His sophism is not unrelated to his previous role as chef, for the Greeks and Romans valued and even enjoyed a good deception from the kitchen. The grammarian Athenaeus, after telling the story of a cook who fooled a king by making turnips taste like anchovies, states that cooks and poets are similar because both are superb manipulators of the imagination.[59] But Augustine's deception is also a playful warning to the group not to concede anything too quickly, which they have certainly been doing.

One of the things the group learns from this incident is that the concept of living well is not necessarily synonymous with happiness, for it can apply not only to those who are truly happy, but to those who are on their way to being happy but are currently miserable. Navigius suspected as much when the group concluded that an unclean spirit cannot seek God. If an unclean spirit cannot seek God, then no one can, for a person with a clean spirit already "has" God and therefore is incapable of seeking Him (one cannot search for what one has already found). And are not the members of this very group "unclean" to a certain extent, still struggling with their own sins and ignorance, and are they not seeking God nonetheless? If the first two of Augustine's propositions above are true, the third becomes problematic.

Everyone laughs at being duped but Monica, the only character who does not understand what has happened. Navigius, who has a more worldly orientation than Monica,[60] came closest to detecting the fallacy, but Monica did not grasp it even after it was revealed. Her piety may have enabled her to master the stronghold of philosophy (see 2.10), but it does not equip her with every philosophical tool or change the nature of her intellectual talents. It does, however, liberate her from that desire to be seen well by others which is so hampering Licentius's progress. Monica is not ashamed to ask Augustine to explain matters that she does not understand; she would rather publicly admit her ignorance and obtain wisdom than hide her ignorance and never grow wise. Such integrity, which availeth much, is also evident later on when Augustine forces Monica to assent to a statement that she does not like. "If reason compels this conclusion," she replies, "I can't deny it" (3.21). Pious Monica respects the power of reason and does not see how its proper use can in any way be inimical to her faith.

Divine Favor Versus Divine Presence (3.20–22)

After being apprised of the fallacy that provoked the group's laughter, Monica changes her position to (1) everyone has God, the unhappy as well as the happy; and (2) those who live well have God "well-disposed" to them (the word here is *propitius*, an adjective commonly applied to the divine in both pagan and Christian Latin).[61] It should be noted that Monica's new position is not Augustine's. Augustine, who equates "having" God with "seeing" God, would be more likely to say that God has everyone rather than that everyone has God (see the last line of 4.34). But for the sake of fanning and cultivating their intellectual *eros*, Augustine is content with facilitating the discussion by pointing out the difficulties in the group's various formulations.

The group struggles to affirm two truths without contradiction: that God is pleased with people seeking Him, and that mere searchers are not yet happy. To this end they introduce several new distinctions: "well-disposed" and "whom He favors" versus "hostile" or "against"; "having God" versus "not being without God"; and lastly, some unnamed condition in between. The group is encountering difficulty because they are essentially being confronted with the enigma of divine presence, that is, the way or ways in which God, who is "utterly hidden and utterly present,"[62] is present to His creation even when His creation is not present to Him. It is a problem of which Augustine is well aware and with which he struggled for some time before reading the books of the Platonists. The *Confessions* gives eloquent testimony to that struggle (and its resolution), but the theme is made explicit early in Augustine's writings. In *On the Immortality of the Soul*, which was originally intended to form a third book of the *Soliloquies*, Augustine contrasts humanity's ontological and beatific relations to God. All, he notes, are possessed by God insofar as they exist, even if they have varying degrees of "closeness" to Him: "Because [the soul] has wisdom from turning toward (*conversio*) that by which it exists, it can lose wisdom by turning away (*aversio*) from that by which it exists. . . . But it cannot lose [its existence], which it has from that of which there is no contrary [God]" (12.19).

More can be said on this topic, but for now it suffices to note that even though the group eventually reaches a tenable solution by the end of 3.21, their confusion bespeaks the need for a philosophically enriched notion of presence, one that properly differentiates the kinds of presence that are conditioned by space, time, and matter from the kinds that are not.

The Lacuna (3.22)

Augustine is ready to move to a new point, although he is apprehensive that the group will be disturbed by it. "Very well," he states, "but I still fear that what we had granted above may disturb you — that whoever isn't happy is miserable, from which it will follow that a man is miserable who. . . ." The text stops abruptly here, for there is a lacuna in the manuscript, one that existed even in Augustine's own lifetime. The *Retractations*, written decades later, states that the lacuna's size is not negligible yet not so great as to constitute a major loss.[63] As I argue in greater detail elsewhere,[64] I believe that three parts are missing: (1) the rest of the paragraph that begins with "When everyone found this agreeable"; (2) a missing paragraph, no trace of which is left; and (3) a third paragraph that includes as its conclusion the text beginning with "someone happy" and ending with "When all had said that they would most gladly do so, we arose." In these missing parts, Augustine and the group most likely wrestle with the statement that someone who seeks God, even though God is well-disposed to him, is miserable. This is a bitter truth, most likely the one that Navigius suspected in 2.13–15, for it means that despite their best efforts, virtually everyone in the group is miserable. Augustine is therefore understandably apprehensive in mentioning it, as he admits in the opening sentence of 3.22.

As for the rest of the lacuna, I conjecture that the missing conversation also effected a shift from the theme of wanting or wishing (*volo*/*volere*), which has framed the discussion of fulfillment so far, to that of needing (*ego*/*egere*), which dominates the rest of the dialogue. During this shift the group apparently agrees with the statement that every person in need is miserable, while Monica concludes that misery is nothing other than need (see Augustine's summary in 4.23, which I contend is a summary of these missing passages). Augustine illustrates one of these points with the quotation from Cicero, which implicitly contrasts having virtue and lacking or needing it and continues the dialogue's comparison of bodily attributes to spiritual—in this case, the rich in land are "poorer" than the rich in virtue.

Augustine then moves on to a consideration about whether Monica is right about misery and need, which he plans to do by examining whether every miserable person is in need (4.23ff). However, it is late in the day, and so after making one more allusion to their feast and exciting their hunger by expressing the hope that they will not "develop a distaste" for their table, Augustine postpones the discussion until tomorrow (4.22).

DAY THREE (4.23–36)

The discussion of the third day begins approximately around the same time as the previous two days, but unlike the second day, there are a number of differences. Instead of resuming their usual positions, the group members sit wherever they want, and instead of the baths, the group convenes in a nearby meadow. The new locale and seating arrangement herald a new or different level in the conversation, while a crystal-clear afternoon (apparently it had been cloudy the previous two days) presages the possibility of a breakthrough in intellectual clarity.

Augustine begins by stating that he now has almost all of the concessions from the group that he wants, a statement which implies that he has indeed been guiding the conversation, not simply acting as a helpless pawn of reason or God (or perhaps the answer is both). Augustine wants to return to the earlier concession that everyone in need is miserable in order to determine whether the converse is true—that every miserable person is in need. He explains that if it is, the final plank will be in place, and "we will most perfectly discover who is happy, for it will be he who isn't in need" (4.23). But did we not already determine that he who has God—the joy of man's desire and his ultimate fulfillment—is happy? In a sense, On the Happy Life should have ended on the second day (3.22). Augustine may have an ulterior motive in pressing the discussion further.

Misery and Need (4.24–29)

Trygetius, who has not learned his lesson about avoiding rash concessions, sees no reason to debate whether every miserable person is in need, since it is obvious. Augustine responds with a clever line of reasoning, suggesting that just as not every person who is not buried is necessarily alive, so too not every person who is miserable is necessarily in need. The strange argument again reveals inequalities within the group, as some are more capable of grasping the analogy than others (4.25). At the very least, the incident places renewed emphasis on the importance of thinking attentively and carefully.

Part of that careful thinking involves a more precise determination of what constitutes need in the life of the happy person. Augustine limits needs to those of the soul as opposed to those of the body. Wisdom is more than simply a knowledge of or about the whole; it is a knowledge accompanied by genuine moral and intellectual virtue. In *Against the Academics* Augustine contrasts the "civic" or "political" virtues of average citizens and the genuine or real virtues "that are known only to the few who are wise" (3.17.37). The wise man is the person whose soul has been perfected or completed by virtue, not merely the person who knows the highest things. As such, his bodily needs are irrelevant. If they are met, all the better; if they are not, it is no great loss, since a lack of bodily goods or the presence of bodily troubles (e.g., pain or the specter of death) cannot "break" him (4.25). The wise man does not avoid bodily goods, and he makes good use of them when they are available, as it would be foolish of him not to. But he is not beholden to these goods, and he does not mourn their loss when they disappear. Augustine is not denigrating bodily goods or needs but pointing out that they cannot be the locus of happiness. Happiness is a fulfillment of the soul rather than the body, and the soul's fulfillment comes only from wanting and obtaining incorporeal goods, which "neither the rust nor moth doth consume" and which "thieves do not break through nor steal" (Matt 6:20).

Having gained a specific understanding of the need in question, Augustine can now move to his main objective. The one difficulty in granting that every miserable person is in need is that many people seem to suffer from no need whatsoever and live a life of abundance and yet are miserable nonetheless (4.26). The key to overcoming this obstacle is again the recognition of only one relevant kind of need—that which pertains to the soul rather than the body. An abundance of bodily goods does not fulfill the needs of the soul. Indeed, the more intelligent a soul is, the more it knows that all of its bodily possessions are subject to the vicissitudes of chance and the more worried it becomes. Borrowing from Cicero, Augustine and Licentius speculate on the peace of mind of Sergius Orata, an intelligent yet greedy man who, on account of his great wealth, had much to lose.

At this point Augustine feigns confusion, concluding that not every miserable person is in need after all, since being afraid or worried is not the same as being in need (4.27). It is Monica who reconciles the apparent discrepancy. The fear of losing one's worldly fortune is the result of inordinately loving a worldly fortune in the first place. Inordinately loving a worldly and ephemeral fortune, in turn, comes from being foolish, specifically, from foolishly thinking that these trinkets matter. The fear of losing unshareable goods, then, is symptomatic of a need, the need for wisdom. Such a need is more than metaphorical, Monica points out, for just as a lack of bodily goods like silver and money can be called a need, so too can a lack of spiritual goods (4.27). At the heart of Monica's insight is again a comparison or analogous understanding of body and soul and the things pertaining to each.

Augustine is thrilled with his mother's remarks, as he was going to make a similar observation, which he had borrowed from the philosophers, as part of a grand finale. He commends Monica as the model of "a mind utterly attentive to God," in contradistinction to a mind immersed in "a myriad of various doctrines" (4.27).

Significantly, his contrast does not juxtapose a lover of wisdom (or philosopher) to a lover of God, as if these were two mutually exclusive categories; nor does he mention someone who is familiar with various philosophical doctrines but who may not love wisdom itself, like a sophomoric student of philosophy. Rather, he compares a mindless collection of (presumably) philosophical doctrines to a mind alive to the presence of God. Such a contrast highlights the importance of a certain presence or mindfulness of the soul as well as the importance of God as the end toward which all sound philosophical teachings are oriented.

The Mind's Need (4.28–29)

Augustine is now in a position to answer in the affirmative that every miserable person is in need just as every needy person is miserable, for every miserable person is in need of wisdom, which alone makes humans happy. With this in mind, Augustine turns to a question about the case of Sergius Orata that had not yet been raised. What if, instead of having a keen intellect that made him aware of the "wavering uncertainties" of this world (4.28), Orata had been a dolt who made his way through life cheerfully oblivious to its many dangers? Would this not be proof of the old adage that where ignorance is bliss, 'tis folly to be wise? Augustine's response is that ignorance and bliss are a contradiction in terms. Happiness is the result of the perfection of the human soul, while ignorance and folly are deficiencies of the soul. Orata therefore would have been an even more miserable wretch if he had been too stupid to see the fragility of his position. It is important to recall again that happiness is not synonymous with pleasant emotions. A lunatic in an insane asylum may be continually pleased by his delusion that he is Napoleon, but no one in his right mind would want to trade places with him. A deficiency that alienates oneself from reality also distances oneself from an authentically happy life.

The Person Without Need (4.30–33)

Faithful to the order he proposed in 4.23, Augustine now considers the person who is not in need. To do so, he introduces a flurry of opposites and etymologies, all of which can be traced to two fundamental notions: being and nonbeing (see 4.30, 4.31). Light and darkness, dress and nakedness (4.29), wisdom and folly, frugality and worthlessness (4.30), wealth and poverty, fullness and need (4.31): each is a pairing of two things, one of which exists by virtue of what it is, the other by virtue of what it is not (and hence there is a way in which the latter does *not* exist more than it does). Augustine's explicit purpose in this fast-paced discourse is to arrive, through the notion of fullness and being, to the nature of *modus*, or measure, which will prove key to understanding wisdom and which "fills" the human soul and eliminates its need. But to have his reader arrive there with him, Augustine must try to trigger, with the help of numerous examples and an almost circular repetition, an insight into the fundamental ontology supporting his conclusions. Such an insight—or rather, two such insights—will not occur through a mere assent to a series of propositions. What is required is an intellectual conversion in which the reader's mind turns to and "sees" for itself what is really real and what is not.[65]

Two Kinds of Knowing (4.29–31)

The intellectual conversion that understands being and nonbeing involves two utterly different kinds of insights that Augustine later in his life designates as knowing according to the form or essence of a thing (*notitia secundum speciem*) and knowing according to privation (*notitia secundum privationem*).[66] The latter, which is essential to an understanding of nonbeing, is especially elusive because it involves knowing that there is nothing knowable about the object in question: some crucial component of "knowability" is intrinsically missing from it. Knowing according to privation, in other words, is knowing that something by its very nature lacks a certain intelligibility. When I know an irrational number, I am knowing a number that lacks what reason (*ratio*) requires in order to comprehend its value completely. When I experience cold, I am experiencing a deprivation in heat. When I understand folly, I understand not a determinate content but the absence of that determinate thing which is called wisdom.[67] When I see darkness, I am "seeing" the absence or privation of light.[68] When I grasp nakedness, I am grasping that there is a shortage of clothing. When I know evil, I am understanding not a good but the privation of a good.[69] And when I know or understand the vice of worthlessness, or *nequitia*, I am knowing or understanding a privation of the virtue of frugality.

As these examples attest, that which is grasped by *notitia secundum privationem* is not nothing generically but nothing with respect to a particular intelligibility that is naturally anticipated by the mind but absent. Hence, these curious "things" are not the mere *absence* of being but the *privation* of a particular kind of being: an irrational number is not the absence of memory, nor is folly the absence of number. What the character Reason says in the *Soliloquies* about falsehood can be applied to the entire category: "A thing which does not exist at all can't even be called false. For if it's false, it exists [as a privation of the true]: if it doesn't exist, it's not false" (2.15.29).

Augustine is aware of the difficulty in coming to terms with insights into privations and the realities—or rather, unrealities—that those insights grasp. In his brief exchange with Trygetius, he speaks of the peculiarity of saying that one "has need" of something, for "having" implies possession but "need" denotes absence. One is therefore compelled to stretch the boundaries of language by making statements like "he has not having" (4.29). But Augustine realizes that knowing according to privation is a small but crucial part of what it means to be wise, for these highly counterintuitive insights often presage significant breakthroughs in the fields in which they occur. Greek geometry would not have progressed far without the discovery of π or the Pythagorean theorem, the former being an "irrational" number—a number lacking the fullness of *ratio,* or intelligibility—and the latter presupposing an understanding of incommensurable lengths, which are likewise irrational. And Augustine would never have left the restrictive compound of materialist dualism for an adequate metaphysics without his realization that evil is not a substance but the privation of a substance.[70] It is because of the importance of *notitia secundum privationem* that three of the four Cassiciacum dialogues contain discussions on specific kinds of privative nonbeing.[71] Mention of this darkness, Augustine declares in *On Order,* sheds much light (2.4.11).

Perhaps it is Augustine's desire to illustrate these peculiar insights that accounts for his stark contrast between folly, which he defines as the "neediness of the mind" (4.28) and wisdom, the fullness of the mind (4.31). Although Plato would grant a sort of mean between the two in the form of right opinion,[72] Augustine denies any such middle ground (4.28). Augustine's dichotomizing of wisdom and folly aptly highlights the manqué nature of folly and, by extension, the significant difference between knowledge according to privation and knowledge according to form.

Measure and Wisdom (4.32–33)

If understanding folly requires an understanding of what is not, understanding wisdom requires an understanding of what truly is. In paragraph thirty-one, Augustine begins a more direct consideration of the positive content of knowledge according to form, at least the instances of knowledge that shed light on the nature of wisdom. He moves from frugality, which is fruitful and hence full rather than stingy and empty (4.31), to moderation and temperance, which are likewise perfectly full, having neither more nor less than they require (4.32). Emerging from this perfect and precise fullness is the notion of measure, or *modus*. Both excess and deficiency lack or are in need of measure, and therefore both are examples of neediness. In the case of the mind or soul, its excessive vices include luxuries, despotism, and pride, and its deficient or "constricting" vices include baseness, fear, sorrow, and lust (4.33).

But the perfect measure of the mind, when the mind is neither empty nor overflowing, is wisdom (4.32). Wisdom, Augustine tells the group, "is none other than the measure of the mind, that is, that by which the mind balances itself, the result being that it neither runs over into excess nor is it constricted by what is less than full" (4.33). Augustine knows that this is an odd definition. It is largely heuristic, which is to say that it merely identifies a known unknown, a reality that is known to exist but the full properties or essence of which have yet to be entirely worked out.[73]

Odd too are the things that Augustine lists when this measure of the mind is not reached or is exceeded, for example, fear and luxury. One would have thought that wisdom would have been contrasted with intellectual failings rather than moral vices, but three considerations must be borne in mind. First, the group's goal is to identify the happy life, which entails the rectification or moderation of one's appetites and desires; it is therefore fitting that the segue to wisdom be moral virtue. Second, even when wisdom is defined primarily as an architectonic form of knowledge, a knowledge that grasps or orders the whole, it is still not divorced from the moral life. Augustine can assume that his interlocutors will agree

with him that a foolish soul is vice-laden and that indeed all of the
soul's vices are a kind of folly (4.30), for he is working within a
particular philosophical and religious tradition in which certain
basic tenets can be presupposed. There is a Platonic-Ciceronian
pedigree to Augustine's claims, but they are also biblical, where
wisdom is intrinsically tied to a good moral condition (see Jas 3:14–
17). Such a view is logically consistent, for a person who knows the
whole knows the good, and a person who acts viciously despite
knowing the good is in some way a fool. Therefore, such a person
cannot be truly wise. Third, Augustine begins but does not end with
the moral dimension of wisdom. He concludes this section with a
description of wisdom as the content of what one would know if
one could transcend the "mirage of images" and behold Being in its
entirety (4.33). Such a vision of the whole would indeed fulfill,
complete, and perfect the mind, answering its every question and
satisfying its every yearning. And by speaking of a move beyond the
Protean images of sensible reality, Augustine is also indicating that
genuine wisdom requires a proper distinction between the sensible
and the intelligible, between what can be grasped by the five bodily
senses and what can be grasped by the mind or intellect alone.
Wisdom is most certainly a knowledge according to form that is
arrived at through intellectual conversion.

Divine Revelation (4.34–35)

At this point Augustine shifts gears to a consideration of the
same notions in light of "divine authority" (4.34). He has no need
here to work out a theory of nature and grace or the differences
between the natural and the supernatural. For his purposes, it is
enough to demonstrate the compatibility of faith and reason by
showing how the tenets of faith aid rather than thwart or co-opt
reason in its quest to know, and how reason does not cease its

activities in light of faith but continues them on a heightened
level.

From divine revelation, Augustine points out, we know that
the Son of God is both Wisdom and Truth, and we know that the
Son comes from the Father and the Father comes from no one. We
also know from reason that truth or wisdom come not from this or
that measure (the measure of fullness, the measure of frugality,
etc.) but from supreme measure, that is, the ultimate notion of
measure from which all other notions of measure are derived. This
supreme measure is itself not measured but rather enables all
other measure to exist. Coordinating these two sets of insights,
Augustine concludes that the Father is the Supreme Measure and
the Son, who is begotten by Him, is Wisdom and Truth (4.34). The
Holy Spirit, in turn, is *Admonitio* (a Latin translation of "Paraclete"),
who admonishes the mind to return to Truth and thence to
Measure. Augustine, continuing his coordination of what is known
by reason and revelation, depicts Admonition as that which pleads
with us to remember God and which brings us to every truth. The
Paraclete is not the Son, that is, He is not "the light that enlighte-
neth every man that cometh into this world" (John 1:9), but He
is the one who pours this light into the eyes of our mind, enabling
us to know. Nor is He begotten by Truth or Supreme Measure,
yet He proceeds from them and is equally "the most almighty
God" (4.35).

Augustine has thus proceeded from relatively mundane notions
such as measure, truth, and admonition to the inner workings of,
and real distinctions within, the Trinity. He has done so by a series
of logical equivalences, yet his critics might suspect him of a series
of equivocations, where the meaning of a word is changed midstream.
Certainly, those who reject the truth claims of Christianity will be
likewise inclined to reject these passages.

It is possible that Augustine is guilty of equivocation, but it is also fair to ask whether he is substituting meanings or whether instead he is teasing out the full implications of those meanings. For instance, can one really have a "mundane" definition of truth, or is the only really adequate definition of truth one that encompasses the realms of metaphysics and epistemology? We have already noted that Augustine is employing a Platonic method whereby realities are viewed in light of their highest principles. In this respect, he is merely amplifying a Platonic strategy by defining the highest not in terms of what is highest for us but what is highest in itself.

Augustine is also presupposing that the teachings of Christianity are true because he is doing not philosophy but what would eventually be called theology, which is grounded in an unquestioned belief in the veracity of the articles of the orthodox Christian faith as it seeks a deeper understanding of them. It is important to note that Augustine presents his Trinitarian reflections as something that happens to make sense of the human condition rather than as a series of rationally demonstrable deductions. He does not endeavor to prove on a strictly logical basis a necessary link between the mind and the Trinity but to show how such a link as he has conceived it with the help of divine authority "fits" or is compatible with the conclusions that the group has already drawn. One may even go so far as to assert that these passages are "plausible" or "probable" in the Academic skeptic's sense of those terms, that is, capable of being approved even if they cannot be grasped with noetic certainty.[74]

The lynchpin to Augustine's plausible theological project, which he does not cite explicitly, is that humans are made in the image of God (Gen 1:27). Since the human mind contains or rather is this image,[75] and since God is revealed as Trinity, it is not unreasonable to conclude that every human mind bears a Trinitarian stamp. Yet this stamp cannot be understood in a spatiotemporal or material way, for the mind itself is an immaterial reality.[76] The mystery of the Trinity can, however, be understood in terms of the mind's activities, albeit dimly. And is it not the case, Augustine would ask his readers, that there is some kind of internal, mental admonition or prompting that leads us to truth, and that the grasp of truth is in some way a grasp of right measure? Such a pattern, it may be added, bears a resemblance to the divine persons as they are portrayed in the New Testament, with the Holy Spirit leading us to the Son (John 16:13–15) and the Son leading us to the Father (John 14:6). Augustine is not dogmatically wed, however, to the analogy that he offers here: he has others in *Against the Academics* and *On Order,*[77] and he will offer something noticeably different decades later in *On the Trinity.* Throughout these shifting paradigms, however, Augustine remains consistent in adhering to the principle that the *imago Dei* in which humans are made must somehow be spiritual rather than corporeal and that it must somehow be Trinitarian.

Augustine's explanation of the mind's trinity, then, is an emphasis on the profound relationship between the knowing subject and its creator, specifically, that *every* act of human knowing (and not just religious or mystical insights) is somehow grounded and participating in the luminosity of God.[78] As Augustine puts it in *Against the Academics,* "only some deity could show man what's true" (3.6.13). Neither a pantheist notion of the mind as God nor a deist notion of the mind as a mechanism that can work on its own once its maker has set it in motion, Augustine's analogy of measure, truth, and admonition to Father, Son, and Holy Spirit presupposes that God is utterly near yet utterly transcendent as pure intelligibility; and the mind, in seeking understanding, participates dynamically in that intelligibility. Moreover, this analogy may indirectly make sense of a specific conundrum that has perplexed the group: how one can both have and have not God (3.20–22). The mind that is admonished to seek the truth is moved by and "has" the spirit of admonition, but it does not "have" the truth. Therefore, it has the Third Person of the Trinity (the Holy Spirit) but not yet the Second (the Son).[79]

Lastly, we have seen several times how Augustine has been trying to fan or explore intellectual *eros*. That double effort continues into these passages: his contrast of fullness and need, wealth and poverty, is a reworking of Diotima's myth in Plato's *Symposium* about *Eros* being the lovechild of *Penia* (Poverty) and *Poros* (Resourcefulness) (4.31). We are now in a position to surmise what — or more properly who — can fulfill this *eros*. One of the purposes of *On the Happy Life* is to show that there is a way in which we are led to know God by our mind's natural longing for Him. Such a longing, as one of Augustine's philosophical sources puts it, is established by the mind's likeness to what is higher than it and by the possibility of attaining a greater resemblance to the higher.[80]

Not Happy Yet (4.35)

After completing his Trinitarian reflections on the human mind, Augustine now returns to the bitter truth that Navigius suspected in 2.13–15 and that Augustine may have mentioned in the missing passages of the manuscript.[81] It must be admitted, he says forthrightly, that we have not yet been filled up by truth or reached this measure, and therefore we are neither wise nor happy. Further, since we are neither wise nor happy, we are, by our own definitions, both miserable and foolish.

Such conclusions should be depressing news for a group that has spent three days in search of the happy life, and yet there is no sign that their spirits have been dampened. Augustine has tempered the unsavory news with two sweet truths, namely, (1) that we now know what the truly happy life is, which is an important first step in its ultimate attainment; and (2) that we not only know what the right target is, but the target itself is actively helping us to reach it. "God is now helping us," Augustine reminds the group, to know the Holy Spirit who leads us to the Truth in order for us to be united to the Supreme Measure.[82] Monica, making her final contribution to the discussion, adds that this gracious aid takes the form of what have come to be known as the three theological virtues: "a firm faith, a lively hope, and an ardent charity" (4.35). Faith, hope, and charity do not circumvent the mind's search for wisdom and happiness but increase its ability to reach its goal (Augustine will discuss this point more concretely in *Soliloquies* 1.6.13). Wretched fools infused with the grace of God and a trust in Him are on their way back to Him. Maybe there is something in between folly and wisdom after all.

Monica's Song (4.35)

Monica, who presumably has been periodically puzzled during this lofty theological discourse, suddenly understands the relevance of what she is hearing by recalling an Ambrosian hymn etched in her memory by frequent use. She may not have fully understood those verses before (like Licentius's parroting of tragic verse in *Against the Academics* 3.4.7?), but her pious practices have preserved them in her mind, thereby paving the way for an insight now. That insight, which correctly identifies the Trinitarian dimensions of Augustine's speech, is described as an "awakening" to her faith (4.35). In response to this epiphany Monica utters the last verse of the hymn, "Cherish, O Trinity, those who pray."

Although it is likely that Monica sang rather than recited the verse, we cannot be certain because of Augustine's unusual diction. He reports that she "poured forth" (*effudit*) the verse. *Effundere* is the same verb that is used in the Latin biblical translations of Jesus's proclamation during the Last Supper: "This is my blood of the new testament, which shall be shed (*effundetur*) for many unto remission of sins."[83] Appropriately, Augustine is establishing a faint verbal link between a hymn used for sacred worship and the Eucharistic feast, the center of Christian worship.

But the verb "to pour forth" also suggests a pagan libation. Augustine has artfully fused together two aspects of a Greco-Roman drinking party. At the end of the meal and to inaugurate the drinking portion of the evening, a hymn of praise was sung to the gods while a libation was poured out in their honor. The hymn, one ancient chronicler tells us, could be sung by all of the partygoers together, by the partygoers in turns, or by the best singers alone, those who "understood what to do."[84] Monica may or may not have the prettiest voice, but she is the best in piety, and to her goes the honor of praising God in song and offering the concluding summary. But instead of proceeding with a night of heavy drinking, the group disbands, ever observant of the dictates of measure. Christian moderation has replaced pagan debauchery, just as Christian piety has modified and transformed the old customs and manners. Lastly, Monica's libation of a hymn recalls Plato's *Symposium*, when the interlocutors offer libations, sing to the god, and do "the other customary things" (176a). Augustine's three-day celebration of his birthday is not only a Roman banquet, but a philosophical and theological feast.

Conclusion (4.36)

With all his heart Augustine thanks "the supreme and true God the Father, the Lord, the liberator of souls*," for this delightful banquet. His nomenclature is itself delightfully ambivalent: he could be thanking God the Father, who is the Lord and liberator of souls, or he could be thanking God the Father, the Lord (His Son), and the Holy Spirit, who is the liberator of souls. We have here a possibly early instance of what was known in medieval theology as the *communicatio idiomatum* of the persons in the Trinity.

Augustine next thanks his guests for the many presents they have heaped upon him and adds that he has been sated by them. His expression of gratitude, which depicts the last two days as extensions of his birthday, subtly reverses the order of satiety. Augustine—at times the bustling host, chef, waiter, and summoner but always the Socratic guide—is implying that his guests have fed him rather than the reverse. It is a fitting topsy-turvy ending to a topsy-turvy dialogue.

But it is not quite the ending, for Trygetius wants to be fed in this measure every day. Although he speaks of moderation, Trygetius is acting greedily by wanting every day to be a party, and so it appears that he has missed the point. Augustine warns him to redirect his attention not to the merriment they have been enjoying, but to the realities to which it has been pointing, *if* he really does want to return to God. This anticlimactic ending, because it spoils some of the mirth and joy of the moment, is an ominous reminder of the backsliding proclivities of humanity. It is relatively easy to become enthusiastic about the happy life once properly stirred up; putting that into practice over time by cultivating the love of God in all things and above all things is another matter altogether.[85] The group departs, but not with the laughter of the first day (2.16) or the gladness of the second (3.22). Their journey, much of which will be difficult, is far from over.

Why Topsy-Turvy?

At least two issues merit further consideration. First, we have seen how Augustine's feast of words has had a recurring topsy-turvy dimension to it, where positions of "birthday boy" and birthday giver, master and servant, and host and guest are inverted. It remains now to examine the significance of such an inversion. According to a historical reconstruction of the calendar in A.D. 386, Augustine's thirty-second birthday on November 13 fell on a Friday.[86] If this is correct, the dialogue culminates three days later, on the Lord's Day, the Church's privileged occasion for celebrating the Eucharist. And the Eucharist, the Church's most cherished sacred banquet, is likewise a topsy-turvy feast, one in which God becomes the servant and the Host becomes the menu, thereby enabling different human souls to be further incorporated into one mystical body. Fittingly, topsy-turvy elements are found in the biblical account of the Last Supper, such as Christ's washing the feet of His apostles and His statements: "You call me Master, and Lord; and you say well, for so I am. If then I, being your Lord and Master, have washed your feet; you also ought to wash one another's feet" (John 13:13–14). Augustine's assumption of lowly duties, then, is in imitation of his Lord, so much so that his service takes on a Eucharistic quality: his feast of words hearkens to the feast of the sacramentally re-presenced Word, the true food of the soul. (One wonders whether Augustine had in mind the image of the risen Lord making breakfast for His friends after the Resurrection [John 21:1–24].) *On the Happy Life*'s Roman-birthday-banquet-turned-philosophical-symposium also echoes the Christian breaking-of-the-bread.

Such an echo (which is strengthened by Monica's doxological "outpouring") is apposite, for the Eucharist is a pledge and foreshadowing of eternal happiness, where the temporal reception of Christ's precious body and blood prefigures the everlasting enjoyment of His divinity. In the *Confessions*, Augustine defines happiness as "joy in truth" and goes on to say that the truth in question is a divine person.[87] But if happiness is a "having" of the truth (to use the language of *On the Happy Life*) and the truth is Jesus Christ, then

Holy Communion, whereby one receives Christ sacramentally, is somehow a participation in or a move toward happiness. Earlier we commented on how even miserable fools can be joyful knowing that they are, by the grace of God, heading toward the happy life. The Eucharistic dimension of *On the Happy Life* provides a key example of the form that that hopeful life takes.

Moreover, this dimension reinforces the importance of the Second Person of the Trinity in the economy of salvation. As several scholars have noted, the first three Cassiciacum dialogues roughly correspond to the three divine persons. *Against the Academics*, with its discussions on measure, highlights God the Father; *On the Happy Life*, with its ongoing concern for wisdom/truth, highlights God the Son; and *On Order*, with its focus on order and reason, highlights God the Holy Spirit.[88] If this is the case, it is appropriate that the dialogue on the Son would have a Eucharistic overtone. And a Eucharistic overtone amply confirms Augustine's statement in the cover letter that *On the Happy Life* is "more religious" than the other Cassiciacum dialogues.

Body-Soul Comparisons

Second, as we have noted previously, there is a tension between Augustine's declaration that one should never compare the things of the body to either God or the soul on one hand (1.4) and the fact that the entire dialogue is based on a protracted comparison of bodily and spiritual things on the other. Sometimes these comparisons reveal similarities between the body and the soul and sometimes they reveal diverging or conflicting needs. In some cases, what is good for the body (or at least for bodily pleasures) can be detrimental to the soul and vice versa. Bodily diseases, for instance, can paradoxically prompt the soul to live a better life, as in the case of Augustine's own pulmonary illness that necessitated his hasty retirement from a meaningless professional life (1.4). But whether it is by similarity or by contrast, the reader is being invited to understand a spiritual or intelligible reality by comparing it to a bodily reality, in seeming violation of Augustine's declaration in the cover letter.

Why, then, does Augustine ostensibly reject body-soul or matter-spirit pairings before offering such pairings in great detail? Such comparisons are common in philosophical and biblical literature and, as Augustine's etymologies in *On the Happy Life* would indicate, an arguably inescapable part of human language itself (Latin is not the only tongue in which spatial and material terms are used as tropes for the nonspatial and the immaterial). But if this is true, Augustine's statement in the cover letter is all the more inexplicable. The key, it seems, is how Augustine makes these comparisons.[89] Using bodily images or metaphors as metaphors or figures for the soul or God is not necessarily the same as thinking about the spiritual or intelligible as reducible to the body or as some kind of bodily substance. Augustine's extended feast of words avoids the insinuation that the soul is beholden or univocally similar to the body, and in fact his analogous understanding of being discloses a different paradigm. Even if we reason our way from physical realities to intelligible ones (the physical being first in the order of discovery), then that reasoning is possible only because the world of space, time, and matter is a dim imitation of the superior and "more real" realm of intelligible reality (which is first in the order of being). Augustine's analogies, in other words, point to the paradox that the words "feast" or "food" are in some respects more properly applied to the world of *soul* than to the world of body: even though it is customary to state that we are applying these physical terms metaphorically or allegorically to the nonphysical, ontologically speaking it may in fact be the reverse. Augustine's cover-letter statement is therefore a gloss on the proper way to interpret his analogical language.

These are heady matters, of course, and moderation being essential to both body and soul, Augustine waits until his next two dialogues to develop further the difficult distinction between the sensible and the intelligible. *On Order* and the *Soliloquies* await the hungry reader.

TIME LINE

THE PROBABLE CHRONOLOGY OF THE CASSICIACUM RETREAT

For the most part the following chronology is based on the conclusions drawn in Denis J. Kavanaugh's *Answer to Skeptics* and Desiderius Ohlmann's De Sancti Augustini Dialogis.

NOVEMBER 386

7th	8th	9th

The party is said to have arrived a "few days" before the beginning of book one of *Against the Academics* (1.1.4), most likely on one of these dates.

Trygetius and Licentius have read Cicero's *Hortensius* either shortly before or after their arrival and are eager for philosophy (*Against the Academics* 1.1.4).

NOVEMBER 386

10th	11th	12th

[Book one of *Against the Academics*]

[Mostly Augustine, Trygetius, and Licentius take part.]

A stenographer is first used (1.1.4) to record a discussion between Licentius and	The group does chores around the villa and studies book one of the *Aeneid* (1.5.15). A	A recorded discussion is held between Licentius and Trygetius on happiness

continued...

Trygetius on happiness
and the quest for truth
that takes place at an
undisclosed location
"that seemed suitable
for the purpose" (1.2.5).
During the discussion,
Alypius departs for
Milan (1.2.5, 1.4.11,
1.6.16). The group
takes a leisurely stroll
during which many
topics are discussed
(but not recorded)
(1.4.10). Licentius and
Trygetius try to resume
their dispute at dusk,
but Augustine
persuades them to
postpone it until
tomorrow (1.4.10).
They all take a trip to
the baths (1.4.10).

recorded discussion is
held (1.4.11) between
Licentius and
Trygetius on happiness
and the quest for
truth that takes place
near sunset at an
undisclosed location
(1.5.15).

that takes place at
dawn at an undisclosed
location (1.6.16).
Lunch (1.9.25).

NOVEMBER 386

13th	14th	15th

[*On the Happy Life*]

[Augustine, Navigius, Monica, Adeodatus, Lastidianus and Rusticus,
Licentius, and Trygetius all take part.]

[Augustine's birthday]
A light lunch (1.6).
Afterwards, a recorded

Lunch (3.17).
Later in the day, a
recorded discussion is

Because the afternoon
is sunny, the final
discussion on

discussion is held in the bathhouse (on account of the morning mist) concerning happiness as "having" God (4.23).

held in the bathhouse (for the same reason as before [4.23]) on who "has" God (3.17).

happiness is held and recorded in the "little meadow . . . nearby" (4.23). After supper, Licentius chants a verse from the Psalms while answering the call of nature; Monica overhears and disapproves (*On Order* 1.8.22). [This is assuming that book one of *On Order* begins on the 16th; if *On Order* begins on the 17th, the outhouse incident happens on the 16th].

NOVEMBER 386

16th   *17th*   *18th*

[Book one of *On Order*, either on the 16th and 17th or on the 17th and 18th]

[Augustine, Licentius, and Trygetius take part, with a brief appearance by Monica at the end.]

A discussion takes place in the middle of the night in the bedroom that Augustine, Licentius, and Trygetius share (1.3.6) and lasts until the early dawn (1.7.20).

Early in the morning, the group gathers "in the usual place" (probably the baths) and continues their discussion on order (1.9.27). Near the end Monica joins the

continued...

Shortly after, Licentius
and Trygetius rise while
Augustine remains in
prayer. After Monica
and Licentius return
from the outhouse,
Augustine hears him
chanting the same verse
that had gotten him in
trouble with Monica
the night before (1.8.22).
Augustine and
Licentius have a brief
conversation (1.8.22ff).
Augustine rises from
bed, and the group
"renders its daily vows
to God" (a possible
allusion to a primitive
version of Lauds)
(1.8.25).
After prayer and on the
way to the baths, the
group witnesses a cock
fight (ibid.).
Once at the baths, they
write down all that
transpired that day
(1.8.26).
Before supper, they
read half a book of
Vergil and do nothing
else for the day (ibid.).

group (1.11.31). The
discussion is the only
business that Augustine
does on this day
(1.11.33).

NOVEMBER 386

20th	*21st*	*22nd*

[Or possibly the 19th, 20th, and 21st]

[Books two and three of *Against the Academics*, which take place on three consecutive days (2.4.10, 2.11.25, 3.1.1) about seven days after the end of book one (2.4.10)]

[Augustine, Licentius, Trygetius, Navigius, and Alypius take part.]

A beautiful clear day; Alypius has returned from Milan at some point (2.4.10). The group arises early and does a small amount of farm work (2.4.10). In the field, the group walks about as the first discussion is read to Alypius, an activity that takes up most of the late morning (2.4.10). While on the way back to the villa, a recorded discussion is held (2.4.10). Lunch at the villa (2.5.13). After lunch, a recorded discussion is held in the field (2.6.14). At sunset the discussion ends, and all return to the house (2.10.24).

An equally pleasant and calm day (2.11.25). Augustine spends the day writing letters (2.11.25), Trygetius reveling in Vergil's poems, and Licentius in writing or studying verse (3.1.1). Two hours before night, a recorded discussion is held in the meadow near the "usual tree" (2.11.25). At darkness all return to the house (2.13.30).

The weather is too gloomy for the meadow, so the bathhouse is chosen for a recorded discussion (3.1.1). (Earlier, Licentius had been singing verses from "Greek tragedies" that he did not understand [3.4.7].) Lunch at the villa (3.3.6). Licentius leaves early, returns to the bath-house, and works more on his verses (3.4.7). Discussion at the bathhouse is resumed (3.4.7). At dusk a lamp is fetched so the recording can continue (3.20.44). At night the discussion comes to a close (3.20.44–45).

continued...

NOVEMBER 386

22nd	*23rd*	*24th*

[Book two of *On Order*, beginning either the day after the last discussion of *Against the Academics* or shortly thereafter, most likely the 23rd, but possibly the 22nd or 24th]

A warm day invites Augustine, Licentius, Trygetius, Monica, and Alypius out on the lawn, where Licentius defends his definition of order in a recorded discussion (2.1.1).

At one point of the discussion Licentius leaves and then returns (2.3.10, 2.5.17).

After being summoned by a boy from the house, the group has lunch (2.6.18).

After lunch, a cloudy sky compels the group to reconvene in the bathhouse for a recorded discussion on various topics related to order (2.6.19).

The discussion culminates in Augustine's explication of the liberal arts and closes at night, after a lamp has been fetched (2.20.54).

NOVEMBER 386–JANUARY 387

Day One	*Day Two*	*Day Three*

[Book one of the *Soliloquies*, which takes place either sometime during the other dialogues, when Augustine is alone by himself, or shortly thereafter (see *Retractations* 1.4.1). No mention of the date of book two of the *Soliloquies* is made, but given Augustine's impatience to continue his conversation with Reason, it presumably takes place not long after (see 2.1.1). The *terminus a quo* of the *Soliloquies* is Augustine's birthday on November 13, 386 (see 1.10.17); the *terminus ad quem* is January 6, 387, when Augustine presumably would have returned to Milan to enroll his name as a candidate for baptism. Augustine would be received into the Catholic Church during the Easter Vigil on April 24–25, 387.]

Soliloquies 1.1.1–1.13.23:	*Soliloquies* 1.14.24–	*Soliloquies* 2.1.1–
At an undisclosed location. Augustine and Reason hold a	1.15.30: The next day (see 1.14.25). Augustine and Reason	2.20.36: Presumably on another day (given the conversation of 1.15.30),

discussion, most likely during the day (*Soliloquies* 1.13.23, 1.14.25), which is similar to the meditations Augustine was accustomed to holding at night (compare *Soliloquies* 1.1.1 and *On Order* 1.3.6). The discussion is concluded in order to spare Augustine's health (*Soliloquies* 1.13.23).

At night, as Augustine mentally reviews these things, his mind drifts to the enticements of a woman's charms (1.14.25).

hold a discussion near a tree, possibly the one in the meadow where the group was accustomed to meeting (see *Soliloquies* 1.15.28; *Against the Academics* 2.11.25).

although this is not explicitly stated. At an undisclosed location, Augustine and Reason hold a discussion.

GLOSSARY OF SELECT NAMES

Adeodatus. The only child of Augustine and his unnamed mistress of fifteen years (*Confessions* 6.15.25). Adeodatus, whose name means "given by God," was born in Carthage in A.D. 372. He went with his parents to Italy and remained there with his father and grandmother after his mother was forced to return to Africa. At Cassiciacum Adeodatus was fourteen or fifteen years old; along with Augustine and Alypius, he was there as a catechumen to prepare for baptism. Augustine comments that his son was "more intelligent than many a grave and learned man" (*Confessions* 9.6.14) and that he was "least of us all in age" but had an "intellectual aptitude, if my love does not deceive me, [that] promises something great" (*On the Happy Life* 1.6). *On the Happy Life* is the only Cassiciacum dialogue in which Adeodatus participates; his participation betrays a high regard for moral purity (see *On the Happy Life* 2.12, 3.18). Adeodatus was baptized along with his father by St. Ambrose in Milan on April 24–25, 387; he was also present at Monica's death, accompanied his father back to North Africa, and joined his father's lay community in Thagaste. The later dialogue *On the Teacher* consists of a conversation between Augustine and Adeodatus that is said to have taken place at this time. Adeodatus died of an undisclosed illness around 389, when he was seventeen or eighteen years old (*Confessions* 9.6.14).

Alypius, St. A native of Thagaste, born after A.D. 354 into a family nobler than Augustine's. He became one of Augustine's students and followed him into the Manichaean sect (*Confessions* 6.7.11–12). According to Augustine, Alypius went on to become a courageous and conscientious lawyer (*Confessions* 6.10.16). He converted to Christianity moments after Augustine, taking and reading the same epistle from St. Paul that prompted Augustine's conversion (*Confessions* 8.12.30). He has a cardinal role to play in *Against the Academics* and *On Order* and is even significant in absentia in *On the Happy Life*. Described as somewhat short and stout (*On the Happy Life* 2.16), Alypius is the closest to an intellectual peer that Augustine has at Cassiciacum. Later he serves as a sort of assistant editor of the Cassiciacum dialogues (see *Against the Academics* 1.1.4; *Confessions* 9.4.7). A close friend of Augustine, who calls him his "heart's brother" (*Confessions* 9.4.7), Alypius eventually became the bishop of Thagaste and died sometime around 427 or 428. Although he is not commonly known as such, Alypius is considered a saint in the Catholic Church. For his feast day on August 15, the *Roman Martyrology* states: "At Tagaste in Africa, St Alipius, Bishop, who was of old a disciple of blessed Augustine, and afterwards his fellow-convert, his colleague in the pastoral office, a gallant fellow-warrior in his contests against the heretics, and lastly his consort in heavenly glory."

Ambrose of Milan, St. The bishop of Milan, Ambrose is called "our priest" by Augustine in *On the Happy Life* (1.4 and 4.35; see also Ambrose, *On Jacob and the Happy Life* 10.43). Elsewhere Augustine calls him "famed among the best men of the whole world" (*Confessions* 5.13.23). As the consular governor of Liguria and Aemilia, Ambrose addressed the Catholic faithful of Milan in order to resolve a dispute as to who should succeed their recently deceased bishop. While he was delivering an eloquent speech on the importance of peace and moderation, the congregation demanded that he be made their bishop (even though he was only a catechumen), and so Ambrose was baptized and ordained in a period of eight days. He went on to become a strong defendant of orthodox Christianity from the Arian heresy and the encroachment of civic power on the affairs of the Church (see *Confessions* 9.7.15–16). From him Augustine learned at least two important lessons: the figurative reading of Scripture (*Confessions* 5.14.24) and the Christian teaching on the immateriality of God's essence (*Confessions* 6.3.4). Monica also held Ambrose in high regard (see *Confessions* 6.1.1–6.2.2); his effect on her piety is evident in *On the Happy Life* 4.35.

Lartidianus. Also known in some manuscripts as Lastidianus. Along with Rusticus, Lartidianus is described as a cousin of Augustine who never had to endure "even a single grammar school teacher" but whose common sense Augustine considered indispensable to the undertaking of *On the Happy Life* (1.6). Lartidianus and Rusticus appear only in *On the Happy Life*, the least philosophically demanding of the Cassiciacum dialogues, and although they participate in the discussion, neither has a recorded line (see *On the Happy Life* 2.12). Nothing else is known of them.

Licentius. The son of Romanianus and thus a relative of Augustine and a native of Augustine's hometown of Thagaste in North Africa. At Cassiciacum he is described as an *adulescens*, a young man somewhere between the ages of fifteen and thirty. Licentius is one of Augustine's two pupils and a principal participant in the dialogues. He is bold and impetuous, with a newfound passion for poetry (*Against the Academics* 2.3.7; *On Order* 1.2.5) and an equally recent but sporadic passion for philosophy (*Against the Academics* 1.1.4, *On Order* 1.3.8–1.4.10). Around A.D. 395, fewer than ten years after their retreat together, Licentius sent Augustine a poem he had composed praising their time at Cassiciacum and asking for further guidance. In his response, Augustine chides his former pupil for still missing the point about the right relationship between the love of wisdom and the love of poetry (see *Epistle* 26).

Monica, St. Augustine's remarkable mother. Possibly a native North African, she married a Roman named Patricius and bore him three children: Augustine, Navigius, and a daughter whose name we do not know. Although her husband was not a Christian at the time, Monica made sure that Augustine was initiated into the catechumenate the moment he was born (*Confessions* 1.11.17). Monica bore Patricius's marital infidelities and bad temper with patience and eventually brought him into the Catholic Church before he died around A.D. 370–371. Although she was initially preoccupied with Augustine's worldly prospects (*Confessions* 2.3.8), she grew more concerned about his spiritual welfare as he fell into debauchery and the Manichaean heresy. Monica prayed for her son constantly, followed him to Italy despite his efforts to evade her, and pestered at least one bishop for help in bringing back her wayward son (see *Confessions* 3.12.21). In the *Confessions*, Augustine credits his embrace of the Christian faith to her intercession (5.7.13, 5.8.15, 5.9.17); in the Cassiciacum dialogues, he writes that he owes everything to her (*On the Happy Life* 1.6) and praises her for her philosophical zeal (*On the Happy Life* 2.10; *On Order* 1.11.32, 2.1.1), for having "a mind utterly attentive to God" (*On the Happy Life* 4.27), and for having a soul "aflame for things divine" (*On Order* 2.1.1). Monica figures prominently in *On the Happy Life* and to a lesser extent in *On Order*; but having little patience for exhaustive epistemological debate (see *On the Happy Life* 2.16), she has only a brief and rather comic cameo, so to speak, in *Against the Academics* 2.5.13. Monica lived to see her son and grandson baptized on April 24–25,

387; shortly after, she succumbed to a deadly fever as she and her family waited in the Roman port town of Ostia for passage back to Africa. She was fifty-six years old.

Navigius. Augustine had at least two siblings, one of them a sister. Little is known of his brother Navigius other than that he was present at Cassiciacum with Augustine (see *Against the Academics* 1.2.5, *On Order* 1.3.7) and later at Ostia when their mother died, where he displayed a somewhat worldly concern for his mother's burial arrangements (*Confessions* 9.11.27). Most likely he accompanied Monica when she followed Augustine to Italy around A.D. 385. Nothing is known of Navigius's education, but he appears to have been more well read than his cousins Lartidianus and Rusticus, showing a familiarity with some of Cicero's writings and an intellectual wariness around Augustine (*On the Happy Life* 2.14).

Romanianus. A relative of Augustine (*Epistle* 26) and his most generous patron. At Carthage he funded Augustine's studies and provided him with a home (see *Against the Academics* 2.2.3); at Milan he enthusiastically supported a plan by Augustine, himself, and their friends to live together in community, and he was willing to use his own resources to make it happen (*Against the Academics* 2.2.3; *Confessions* 6.14.24). Many misfortunes had recently befallen Romanianus, which is why Augustine urges him to take these as a sign to study philosophy (see *Against the Academics* 1.1.2; *Confessions* 6.14.24). Augustine tries to repay his debt to his old friend as well as to atone for leading him into Manichaeism (see *Against the Academics* 1.1.3) by dedicating two works to him: *Against the Academics*, a call to the study of philosophy, and the treatise *On True Religion*, an invitation to convert to the Christian faith. Some conjecture that Romanianus accepted at least one of these invitations, possibly converting to Christianity in A.D. 396. As we learn in *Against the Academics* 1.1.4, he is also the father of Licentius, one of the main participants of the Cassiciacum dialogues.

Rusticus. Along with Lartidianus, Rusticus is described as a cousin of Augustine who never had to endure "even a single grammar school teacher" but whose common sense Augustine considered indispensable to the undertaking of *On the Happy Life* (1.6). Lartidianus and Rusticus appear only in *On the Happy Life*, the least philosophically demanding of the Cassiciacum dialogues, and although they participate in the discussion, neither has a recorded line (see *On the Happy Life* 2.12). Aside from his being particularly shy (*On the Happy Life* 2.12), nothing else is known of Rusticus.

Theodorus. Manlius Theodorus (his first name is mentioned in the *Retractations* but not in the Cassiciacum dialogues) was made consul of the Roman Empire in A.D. 399; before that he held several other important administrative offices under several emperors. He was the subject of a panegyric written in verse by the poet Claudian. Augustine asserts in *On Order* 1.11.31 that his mother Monica knew him and that his philosophical works are so erudite that "both now and in the coming generations, no class of men may rightly complain about the writings of our times" (see also *Soliloquies* 2.14.26). In the *Retractations* Augustine reiterates that Theodorus was a "learned and Christian man," though he now regrets having attributed more to him than he should have (1.2). Little is known about the personal acquaintance between Augustine and Theodorus in Milan, as well as how well Monica knew him. Although Theodorus wrote on a variety of subjects, his only extant work is the treatise *On Meters* (*De metris*). Augustine dedicated *On the Happy Life* to him as a way of petitioning him to evaluate his spiritual progress (*On the Happy Life* 1.1, 1.4). It is doubtful that Theodorus ever complied with the request.

Trygetius. One of two pupils of Augustine at Cassiciacum, a fellow townsman of Thagaste, and a principal participant of these dialogues (see *On the Happy Life* 1.6). Trygetius is referred to as an *adulescens*, a youth between the ages of fifteen and thirty. Augustine writes of him in *Against the Academics* 1.1.4: "It is as if military service had conscripted the young man for a while in order to remove his distaste for the disciplines, and so it restored him to us extremely passionate and hungry for the great and noble arts." Given that the average age of a recruit in the Roman army was eighteen or older, he may have been a couple of years older than Licentius. In *On Order* 1.2.5, Augustine again mentions Trygetius's military service and describes him as someone "who has fallen in love with history like an old soldier."

Verecundus. A generous and relatively wealthy friend who lent his villa at Cassiciacum to Augustine and his friends (*Confessions* 9.3.5). A grammarian by profession living and working in Milan, Verecundus may have been part of the circle of friends that desired to live together in a life of philosophical leisure (*Confessions* 6.14.24). When he heard of Augustine's and Alypius's conversions to Christianity, Verecundus not only wanted to convert as well but to join them in leading celibate lives. Verecundus, however, was married (to a Christian woman), and so he reluctantly deferred conversion as Augustine and Alypius encouraged him to remain faithful to his married state. Although he worried that his friendship with the group would suffer, he gladly lent out his villa for their baptismal preparations (*On Order* 1.2.5). Verecundus eventually did convert and died shortly thereafter (*Confessions* 9.3.5).

Zenobius. A mutual friend of Augustine, Romanianus, and Verecundus. Zenobius was the victim of some kind of political or financial misfortune and had been forced to leave Milan (*On Order* 1.7.20), probably northward to the Alps (*Soliloquies* 2.14.26). Augustine portrays Zenobius as a man of outstanding moral character (*On Order* 1.2.4) and a lover and composer of poetry (*On Order* 1.7.20): he wrote a "good poem" about the difficulties of reconciling God's goodness with the existence of evil (*On Order* 1.7.20), as well as a poem that helps conquer the fear of death (*Soliloquies* 2.14.26). Augustine hints, however, that Zenobius is in need of more intellectual formation and philosophical training (*On Order* 2.5.15). Augustine also wrote a brief letter to Zenobius while he was at Cassiciacum (*Epistle* 2).

NOTES

GENERAL INTRODUCTION TO THE CASSICIACUM DIALOGUES

1. "Fruitful leisure": *On Order* 1.2.4; farm work: see *Against the Academics* 1.5.15; violent poultry: see *On Order* 1.8.25; Augustine states that stenographers, possibly hired by Romanianus, were used to record the conversations of the group: see *Against the Academics* 1.1.4, 1.5.15, 1.9.25, 2.7.17, 2.9.22, 3.7.15; *On Order* 1.5.14, 1.7.20, 1.9.27, 1.10.29–1.11.31, 2.20.54; on Augustine's health, see *Against the Academics* 3.7.15; *On Order* 1.2.5; on recording these conversations for those not present, see *Against the Academics* 1.1.4, 1.5.15, 1.9.25, 2.7.17, 2.9.22, 3.7.15; *On Order* 1.2.5, 1.5.14, 1.7.20, 1.9.27, 1.10.29–1.11.31, 2.20.54; on Alypius as collaborating editor, see *Against the Academics* 1.1.4; *Confessions* 9.2.4. Unlike the other three dialogues, the *Soliloquies* is not derived from transcribed conversations but is nonetheless — as I argue in the introduction to the *Soliloquies* — an integral part of the Cassiciacum corpus.

2. See *Soliloquies* 1.1.3.

3. The language of intellectual, moral, and religious conversion is borrowed from Lonergan, *Method*, 238–43. It should be noted that these conversions often overlap, that they do not follow the same chronological order in every case, and that an individual may not necessarily undergo all three.

4. Knowing God and the soul: see *Soliloquies* 1.2.7, 1.15.27, 2.18.32; "return to ourselves": see *Against the Academics* 1.1.1, 2.2.5, 2.3.8.

5. "Inquiry into inquiry": Kenyon, *Augustine*, 30; "look foremost": ibid., 12; "cognitive norms of thought": ibid., 34; "most if not all acts of rational inquiry": ibid., 40.

6. "And what did it profit": *Confessions* 4.16.30, trans. Frank J. Sheed; "the order for living": *On Order* 2.8.25; sharp criticism: see *On Order* 1.10.29–30; Reason's embarrassing questions: see *Soliloquies* 1.14.25–26.

7. On baptism, see *Confessions* 9.3.6, where Augustine refers to his baptism as his *conversio*; on religion as binding, see *On True Religion* 55.111, 113 (in *Retractations* 1.13.9, Augustine notes that although there is some uncertainty regarding the etymology of *religio*, he prefers the interpretation that traces it to *religo*, "to bind"); on Christianity and freedom, see *On True Religion* 17.33; on Monica on faith, hope, and charity, see *On the Happy Life* 4.35.

8. For instance, Robert J. O'Connell, S.J., spent the bulk of his career arguing for a disjunction between an early Augustine imbued with a Neoplatonic, anticorporeal "angelism" and a later Augustine more properly informed by an incarnational Christianity: see O'Connell, *St. Augustine's Early Theory*, *St. Augustine's Platonism*, and *Art*. For a critique of O'Connell's thesis, see Fortin, "Reflections," 99, Review, *Birth of Philosophic Christianity*, 317–19; and Harrison, *Rethinking*.

9. On the necessity of intellectual conversion, see *On Order* 1.8.24 and *Confessions* 4.16.30; on the order of conversions, see *Against the Academics* 3.17.38 and *On Order* 2.8.25–2.9.26.

10. Plato, *Republic* 10.607b.

11. The distinctive traits of the philosophical dialogue are aptly summarized by Cicero, who introduced the genre to Rome: it hides the author's opinion, frees the reader from error, and helps the reader reach the most probable or plausible truth (*Tusculan Disputations* 5.4.11).

12. See Plato, *Phaedrus* 275d–277c. Compare Augustine, *On Christian Doctrine* 4.9.23 and St. Thomas Aquinas, *Commentary on Boethius*, q. 2, a. 4.

13. On the esoteric and exoteric, see Crosson, "Esoteric Versus Latent Teaching." The prevalence or even existence of an esoteric literature was debated in ancient Greece and Rome and again during the Renaissance and early modern period (the Commentary on *Against the Academics* cites several ancient passages on this topic). In the twentieth century the debate was controversially revived by Leo Strauss; the most thorough treatment on the topic to date is Melzer, *Philosophy Between the Lines*. On Augustine, Strauss, and esotericism, see Kries, "Augustine as Defender."

14. On Augustine's conjectures about Academic esotericism, see *Against the Academics* 2.10.24, 3.7.15–3.20.43; on the few versus the many, see *Against the Academics* 1.1.1, 2.1.1, 2.2.6, 3.17.37; *On the Happy Life* 1.1; *On Order* 1.1.1, 1.11.32, 2.5.16, 2.9.26, 2.11.30; *Soliloquies* 1.1.2, 1.1.4, 1.13.22; on the

danger of teaching the truth, see *Against the Academics* 3.17.37; "return to their very selves": *Against the Academics* 3.19.42.

15. On joke-telling, see *Soliloquies* 2.9.16; on Augustine's irony, see *Retractations* 1.3.2; "in sport": *A Dialogue Concerning Heresies*, 69/1–2; "holds as trivial": Cicero, *On Duties* 1.20.67; on the comic structure of philosophical dialogue, see Downey, *Serious Comedy*; on "untruths," see *On Order* 2.14.40.

16. On engrafting, see *On Order* 1.2.4. For the sake of readability, the current translations do not follow the convention of using "he says" in the present tense.

17. See *Against the Academics* 2.1.1; *On the Happy Life* 4.34; *On Order* 1.1.3; *Soliloquies* 1.1.1ff.

18. For Augustine's opinion of Cicero, see *Against the Academics* 1.3.8 and 3.16.36; on Augustine's first encounter with *Hortensius*, see *Confessions* 3.4; on the *Hortensius* at Cassiciacum, see *Against the Academics* 1.1.4; "cedars of the gymnasia" and "Church's wholesome herbs": *Confessions* 9.4.7. It should be noted that Augustine also modifies the Ciceronian dialogue even as he adopts it. One of his most significant changes is rearranging the chronology of a Ciceronian dialogue from (1) aporetic confusion, (2) plausible explanation, and (3) reflection on the act of debating to (1) aporetic confusion, (2) reflection on the act of debating, and (3) plausible explanation. This reordering lends to Augustine's dialogues a more dramatic element similar to that of a mystery novel. See Kenyon, *Augustine*, 13, 77–79.

19. "Living happily": Cicero, *On Divination* 2.1.2; for more on this thesis, see Foley, "Cicero, Augustine"; on boredom after mastery, see *Against the Academics* 3.4.7.

20. On intellectual conversion, see *Confessions* 7.9.13; "When behold": *Against the Academics* 2.2.5.

21. For a summary of the debate on Augustine's familiarity with Plato, see O'Donnell, *Augustine Confessions*, vol. 2, 421–24.

22. See Pucci, *Virgilian Retreat*. Pucci prefers the terms "recuperating" (xiii).

23. On Augustine's literary regrets: Augustine writes in the *Retractations* that he wishes he had not mentioned the Muses and other pagan figures, even though the allusions were not meant to be taken literally (1.3.2), and he laments being "puffed up" with the "conventions of worldly literature" (Prologue, 3). It should be borne in mind, however, that Augustine tells his reader that in the *Retractations* he is approaching his earlier writings with a judgment more exacting and severe than even God's in order to avoid His final judgment (Prologue, 1). Such a hermeneutic has several advantages, but not included among them is giving the benefit of the doubt to possibly

innocuous passages. On fighting fire with fire: In response to accusations like Julian the Apostate's that Christianity was no more than a religion of "theologizing fishermen," Church Fathers such as Minucius Felix endeavored to refute the pagans with their own literary weapons (see *Octavius* 39; see also Jerome, *Epistle* 70.2; Gregory of Nazianzus, *Oration* 43.11).

24. See *On the Happy Life* 4.31–36. These alignments will be discussed in greater detail in the Commentaries.

25. On Ambrose's influence, see *Confessions* 5.13.23, 6.1.1–6.4.6; on Marius Victorinus's influence, see *Confessions* 8.2.3–5.

26. On neologisms, see Bogan, *Vocabulary*, 43; "beatific vision": *Soliloquies* 1.7.14; on cuckoo clocks, see *Soliloquies* 2.6.12.

ON THE HAPPY LIFE
Introduction

1. *Tusculan Disputations* 5.4.10–11.
2. See *Politics* 1323a21–1323b28.
3. *Enneads* 1.4.
4. *On Jacob and the Happy Life* 1.1.
5. *Nicomachean Ethics* 1098b20, 1098a15.
6. See Parry, "Ancient Ethical Theory." An exception to this trend is virtue ethics.
7. See *Nicomachean Ethics* 1101a20.
8. See *Tusculan Disputations* 5.8.22–23.
9. Newman, *Idea*, 91.
10. See Downey, *Desperately Wicked*, 81–89.
11. See *On Jacob and the Happy Life* 9.42ff.
12. See *Tusculan Disputations* 5.2.5–6.
13. See *Tusculan Disputations* 5.1.2.
14. See *Tusculan Disputations* 5.10.30–31.
15. Cicero will eventually find a more satisfactory solution in *On Duties*, where he reconciles the Aristotelian and Stoic positions by characterizing virtue as the right regulation of external goods. By this account the virtuous man "needs" external goods, but only as the raw matter on which to exercise his virtue, not as direct sources of happiness.
16. See *Tusculan Disputations* 5.7.19–20.
17. See *Tusculan Disputations* 5.2.5; *On the Happy Life* 1.1–5.
18. Soul's "food": see *On the Happy Life* 2.8; *Tusculan Disputations* 3.1.1–3.3.6; frugality: see *Tusculan Disputations* 3.8.16–18; *On the Happy Life* 2.8.

19. Always happy: see *Tusculan Disputations* 5.15.43, 16.48; *On the Happy Life* 2.14; soul is perfect: see *Tusculan Disputations* 5.13.37, 38; *On the Happy Life* 4.25; bodily wants: see *Tusculan Disputations* 5.32.90–5.36.105; *On the Happy Life* 4.25; caprices of chance: see *Tusculan Disputations* 5.26.73, 5.37.106–5.40.118; *On the Happy Life* 4.25; strong and unafraid: see *Tusculan Disputations* 5.6.16, 5.27.77–79; Augustine, *On the Happy Life* 4.25; see also *Tusculan Disputations* 3.7.14 for the wise man's strength, *Tusculan Disputations* 1 for his indifference to death, and *Tusculan Disputations* 2 for his indifference to pain.

20. See *Confessions* 5.13.23–5.14.24, 6.3.3–6.4.5.

21. *On the Happy Life* 1.5.

22. See *Confessions* 7.21.27.

23. Coleridge, "Aids to Reflection," 225.

24. Being and nonbeing: see *On the Happy Life* 4.30; Trinity: *On the Happy Life* 4.35.

25. *City of God* 13.20; see also *Literal Meaning of Genesis* 12.35.68.

26. See *Retractations* 1.4.3.

27. Theophrastus was a disciple of Aristotle who, because he held that external advantages such as wealth and health are goods, and because external goods are vulnerable to (mis)fortune, felt compelled to conclude that "life is ruled by fortune, not wisdom" (see Cicero, *Tusculan Disputations* 5.9.24–25).

28. See *Tusculan Disputations* 3.3.6.

29. See *On the Happy Life* 3.17, where Augustine asserts that it is God, not he, who is preparing the meals.

30. See *On the Happy Life* 2.10, 2.14, 2.16, 3.19, 3.21.

31. See *Against the Academics* 2.7.18; see also the laughter at 3.3.6. See *On Order* 1.10.30 versus (arguably) 1.11.33; see also the laughter at 2.6.18.

32. See *Soliloquies* 1.14.26.

33. See *City of God* 4.18.23.

34. See *On the Happy Life* 1.3.

35. See *On the Happy Life* 2.10.

On the Happy Life

1. For the image of philosophy or wisdom as a port, see *Against the Academics* 1.1.1, 1.9.25.

2. See *Against the Academics* 2.2.4: "it seemed to me that no fortune was favorable unless it granted the leisure of philosophizing and no life was happy unless it was lived in philosophy."

3. A more literal translation for *rari admodum paucique* is "rare and very few." On the rarity of philosophical mastery or true philosophers (a common tenet in classical philosophy), see *Against the Academics* 1.1.1, 2.1.1, 2.2.6, 3.7.37; *On Order* 1.1.1, 1.11.32, 2.5.16, 2.9.26, 2.11.30; *Soliloquies* 1.1.2, 1.1.4, 1.13.22.

4. By "necessity" Augustine appears to be referring to Cicero's understanding of fate as "the order and series of causes" (*On Divination* 1.55.125).

5. For more on the surprisingly good value of (at least some) misfortune, see 1.2 and 1.4 below; *Against the Academics* 1.1.1.

6. Augustine's language continues the maritime imagery, but it also hints at Philosophy as a patron receiving her clients. His division of three classes of seamen capable of philosophizing is redolent of Seneca's three classes of people who are to varying degrees free of mental and moral "diseases" (see Seneca, *Epistle* 75).

7. The phrase is borrowed from Cicero, *On the Orator* 1.33.153.

8. In describing the establishment of a lighthouse or lighted buoy as the erecting of a very bright standard or sign (*lucidissimum signum erigere*), Augustine weaves together two different images: that of soldiers raising the battle standard of their division on a hill (see Livy, *History of Rome* 27.48.12; Augustine, *On the Teacher* 4.9; *On Christian Doctrine* 2.3.4), and that of the stars, which have been poetically called "bright signs" (*signa lucida*; see Lucretius, *On the Nature of Things* 5.5.17; Martial, *Epigram* 9.71.7; see also Gen 1:14).

9. The word here for compatriot is *civis*, used elsewhere by Augustine to designate fellow townsmen, in his case, those who hail from his hometown of Thagaste in North Africa (see 1.6 below; *Against the Academics* 1.1.2).

10. Augustine's taxonomy of different seafarers can be compared to the different kinds of spectators he describes in *Soliloquies* 1.13.23. It also harkens to Seneca's description of three kinds of progress: without help, with help, and under the constraint of a guide (see *Epistle* 52.3–4). Categorizing into groups of three was common in antiquity. Varro describes three kinds of life (see Augustine, *City of God* 19.1–2); Ambrose, three kinds of death (*On the Passing of His Brother Satyrus* 2.37); and Servius, three kinds of purification and return of the soul to the body (*Commentary on the Aeneid* 6.741, 6.745).

11. For the use of homeland or fatherland (*patria*) as a symbol for God, see *Against the Academics* 3.19.42; *Soliloquies* 1.1.4. For the return to God, see 4.36 below. Plotinus, from whose works Augustine draws not infrequently, explains that the "fatherland" is "there from where we have come; there is our Father." The admonition from Homer's *Iliad* 2.140 is therefore good

advice: "Let us flee to our beloved homeland" by putting out to sea (*Enneads* 1.6.8). For Plotinus's application of this line to the journeys of Odysseus in the *Odyssey* and for Augustine's use of the *Odyssey* here and in 1.4, see "Taking Sail Against a Sea of Troubles (1.1–2)" in the Commentary.

12. Following Plato, Augustine describes the soul as having three basic kinds of desire: the desire for physical pleasure or physical objects; the desire for honor, glory, prominence, revenge, etc.; and the desire for truth or knowledge. The first two kinds of desire can easily lead the soul away from the third and highest kind. For the winds of fortune, see Cicero, *On Duties* 2.6.19.

13. See Vergil, *Aeneid* 1.3.

14. See *Against the Academics* 3.14.30, where Augustine describes a mass (*moles*) or mountain on which the Academics dwell. See also *Aeneid* 1.159–63, where Vergil describes an island at the mouth of a harbor with high cliffs.

15. See Lucretius, *On the Nature of Things* 2.7–9.

16. For the rocks of this life, see *On Order* 1.1.1. See also Cicero, *Consolation* frg. 9: "It is best by far not to be born, and not to fall upon these rocks of life. But if you have been born, the next best thing is to flee as soon as possible from fortune as if it were a conflagration" (see Lactantius, *Divine Institutes* 3.19).

17. The image of an unstable volcanic surface is reminiscent of Plotinus's description of an ugly, immoral soul commanding nothing but "a life smouldering dully under the crust of evil" and headed toward darkness (*Enneads* 1.6.5).

18. The *Hortensius*, which exists now only in fragments, was loosely based on Aristotle's *Protreptikos*, also lost. In the dialogue, Cicero attempts to persuade Quintus Hortensius Hortalus, an accomplished orator and lawyer known for his defense of corrupt provincial governors, of the superiority of philosophy to sophistical rhetoric in facilitating genuine human happiness. As Augustine testifies in the *Confessions*, the *Hortensius* was an exhortation not to this or that school of thought, but to philosophy itself, that is, to the love of wisdom tout court (3.4.7–8). It had a life-changing effect on him when he read it at the age of eighteen (ibid.; see *Soliloquies* 1.10.17), and it also appears to have had a similar effect on his two pupils (*Against the Academics* 1.1.4).

19. What follows is a description of Augustine's involvement with Manichaeism, a Persian religious sect with which he remained for nine years (see *Confessions* 3.6.10–3.7.14, 5.6.10).

20. The image, which echoes Vergil's *Aeneid* 3.515 (see also Augustine, *On the Usefulness of Believing* 1.2), depicts Augustine's interest as a young man in astrology (see *Confessions* 4.3.4–6) and Manichaean cosmology (ibid., 5.3.3–6, 5.5.9).

21. Literally, when I became more erect. Augustine uses the image of standing upright as a symbol of reason's coming into its own, its ability to rise above obscure or apparently contradictory data and gain a higher, more intelligent viewpoint (see *On Order* 1.1.1).

22. As a Hearer in the Manichaean sect, Augustine was commanded to do strange things, such as pick a fig from a tree and serve it to the more elite members, called the Elect, so that their digestive tracts could release the divine particles contained therein (see *Confessions* 3.10.18). After meeting the Manichaean bishop Faustus, however, Augustine concluded that behind their various orders there was no substantive teaching (see *Confessions* 5.6.10–5.7.13) and that both the Academic skeptics and Catholic teachers such as St. Ambrose had more to offer (see *Confessions* 5.14.25 and 5.13.23–5.14.24, resp.).

23. Although they radically distinguished spirit from matter, the Manichaean sect had an essentially materialist understanding of spiritual reality (see *Confessions* 3.6.10–3.6.11, 3.10.18).

24. The metaphor here is that of a gift-wrapped present. Augustine suspected the Manichaeans of harboring a secret or esoteric teaching that was being concealed by the "wrappings" of their public doctrines (see *Confessions* 3.6.10–11, 6.3.3).

25. Possibly, Augustine's knowledge of astronomy struck down Manichaean astrology (see *Confessions* 5.3.3–5). Drawing from Plotinus, Augustine compares his time with the materialist Manichaeans to Odysseus's imprisonment by the sensualist "sorceries of Circe and Calypso" (*Enneads* 1.6.8); or the comparison may be to Odysseus and Polyphemus the Cyclops.

26. Founded by Carneades (214–129/128 B.C.), the so-called Third or New Academy taught that a knowledge of things can never be attained with certainty. After becoming disenchanted with Manichaeism, Augustine subscribed for a while to this form of skepticism (see *Confessions* 5.10.19). The teaching of the Academic skeptics is the subject of *Against the Academics*.

27. See Augustine, *On the Usefulness of Believing* 8.20.

28. For the metaphor of the North Star as a reliable point by which one can navigate one's life, see Cicero, *Academica* 2.20.66. The North Star referenced here is the Catholic Church: after meeting Ambrose, Augustine

resolved to remain a catechumen in the Church of his parents "until some certain light should appear by which I might steer my course" (*Confessions* 5.14.25).

29. St. Ambrose, bishop of Milan.

30. See *Confessions* 5.14.24, 6.3.4–6.4.6

31. For asterisked words, see the Translation Key.

32. Since the soul is made in the image and likeness of God, it is the one reality in the created world that most closely resembles Him (see Gen 1:26; *Confessions* 3.7.12, 5.10.20, 6.3.4–6.4.5). Augustine also cautions against comparing the sensible and the intelligible in *On Order* 2.15.42.

33. Literally, of a wife and honor (see *Confessions* 6.6.9). Marrying a wealthy or wellborn woman increased one's chances of worldly success. Augustine may also be mentioning his desire for marriage here in order to indicate his enslavement to lust at the time (see *Confessions* 8.1.2).

34. For example, Augustine and several friends resolved to form a community dedicated to the life of contemplation, but once they began to wonder whether their wives would agree to it, the whole plan "fell to pieces in [their] hands" (*Confessions* 6.14.24). The strongest advocate of the plan was Romanianus, to whom *Against the Academics* is dedicated (ibid.; *Against the Academics* 1.1.1).

35. Manuscripts of *On the Happy Life* do not agree on whether the author named here is Plato or Plotinus, although they lean toward the latter. In *Confessions* 7.9.13, Augustine mentions reading the books of the *Platonici*, or "Platonists" (see also *Confessions* 8.2.3; *Against the Academics* 3.18.41).

36. In the *Confessions* 7.9.13–14, Augustine compares the surprising similarities and differences between the books of the Platonists and the prologue to the Gospel of St. John (John 1:1–18). The mysteries are those realities revealed by God through Scripture or liturgy or any other dimension of the Church's sacred tradition (see *Against the Academics* 2.1.1; *On Order* 2.5.15, 2.6.16, 2.9.27, 2.17.46).

37. As Augustine elaborates in the *Confessions*, he was worried that a sudden resignation from his teaching position, so soon before the end of the term, would appear ostentatious and draw undue attention to his and Alypius's conversions (9.2.3).

38. Augustine describes the ailment that forced his retirement from the "burden" of teaching rhetoric as a *pectoris dolor*, a chest pain (here, in *Against the Academics* 1.1.3, and in *Confessions* 9.2.4) and as a *stomachi dolor*, a pain in the gullet or esophagus (*On Order* 1.2.5, 1.11.31). His most detailed account is in the *Confessions*: "My lungs began to give way under

the great hardship [of teaching], and I inhaled with difficulty. And the pains in my chest were witnessing to the fact that my lungs were not well and were keeping me from speaking in a loud voice for a prolonged amount of time. At first this greatly disturbed me, since it was forcing me to cast off, almost now by necessity, the burden of this teaching position—or at least, if I could convalesce and be cared for, to put it off intermittently" (9.2.4; see 9.5.13). This respiratory problem continued to vex Augustine throughout his time at Cassiciacum (see *Against the Academics* 3.7.15; *On Order* 1.2.5, 1.11.33; *Soliloquies* 1.1.1).

39. Aulus Gellius, *Attic Nights* 16.3.16; Arrian, *Discourses of Epictetus* 2.23.36–41.

40. The expression "worn out ship" (*fessa navis*) is Vergilian (see *Aeneid* 1.168, 5.28).

41. That is, like a ship on stormy waters, the question is still being tossed and turned about in Augustine's mind. In the *Soliloquies*, Augustine claims that he does not know the soul, nor can he prove that it is immortal (1.2.7, 2.1.1, resp.).

42. The meaning of "Theodorus" in Greek.

43. In the *Retractations* 1.2 Augustine says that he does not like that he "often mentioned Fortune by name." Elsewhere he elaborates:

> I do not like how many times I mentioned Fortune, although I did not intend by this name for some goddess to be understood but rather a fortuitous occurrence of things (either in our body or in goods or evils outside of us). And hence no religion prohibits the following words from being said: "perhaps" (*forte*), "maybe" (*forsitan*), "perchance" (*fortasse*), "by chance" (*fortuito*). Still, all of these should be traced back to divine providence. Also, I was not silent about this in [*Against the Academics*] but said: "In fact, perhaps what is commonly called Fortune is actually being ruled by a certain hidden order, and what we call chance in human affairs is nothing but something the reason and cause of which are concealed" (1.1.1). I definitely said this, yet I regret using the word "fortune" there in the way that I did, since I see that people hold on to a very bad habit: where one ought to say, "God has willed this," they say, "Fortuna has willed this." (*Retractations* 1.1.2)

Fortuna, the Roman goddess of chance, had many temples in Rome dedicated to her. She was portrayed with a cornucopia (a symbol of the prosperity she bestows) and a ship's rudder (symbol of her control over one's fate). Although *fortuna* was also the word for chance (and thus could be used in a harmless manner), Augustine fears that its pagan derivation could linger, especially when used so frequently.

44. November 13, 386. Augustine was born in A.D. 354, making him thirty-two years old today.

45. More literally, in order that none of our intellectual aptitude (*ingenium*) would be hindered. In the words of a Latin proverb: *Plenus venter non studet libenter*—a full belly does not study gladly. Moderation at meals is a philosophical virtue practiced in a noteworthy way by Socrates (see Xenophon, *Memorabilia* 1.3.5–9).

46. The indoor baths were a suitable location for a discussion because late autumn in northern Italy was often too cold for staying outside (see 4.23 below; *Against the Academics* 3.1.1; *On Order* 1.8.25, 2.6.19). It was not unusual for private Roman bathhouses to be separate buildings or annexes with multiple rooms, warm water, and underfloor heating (see Cicero, *Epistle to Quintus His Brother* 3.1).

47. Literally, by whose merit I am all that I live. Augustine credits not only his earthly existence, but his life in Christ to his mother Monica.

48. See Augustine, *On the Morals of the Catholic Church* 1.4.6; *Confessions* 10.6.9; *Sermon* 150.4–5.

49. For a similar line of questioning, see *Soliloquies* 2.1.1.

50. Augustine has shifted from the body and life to the body and the soul because as the principle of growth, sensation, and appetition, the soul "is the life of bodies" (*Confessions* 3.6.10; see 10.6.10).

51. Perhaps this promise is fulfilled at 4.34 below.

52. For other examples of minds wandering during meals, see *Against the Academics* 2.4.10, 3.4.7.

53. Literally, the good arts. Augustine most likely has in mind not *les beaux arts* of painting, sculpture, etc., but the seven liberal arts.

54. Some forms of mange (a skin disease usually found in livestock) can be caused by malnutrition.

55. The word *nequitia* can also mean wickedness.

56. *Vitia*, translated above as "defects."

57. Unlike *frux*, *fructus* can mean reward or enjoyment as well as fruit.

58. See Cicero, *Tusculan Disputations* 3.8.18. Augustine repeats this etymology in *On True Religion* 11.21.

59. See Cicero, *Timaeus* 3; *Academica* 1.8.31; Plotinus, *Enneads* 1.8.3.

60. One would have expected a more metaphysical example, but if virtue is a perfection of the human soul, and if perfection, to be perfection, admits of

no change, then a truly and fully virtuous soul would possess an excellence that is permanent and stable.

61. Despite its grammatical awkwardness Augustine does not assign a noun to the adjective two (*duo*) that would categorize both the soul and the body. Soul and body are not two different, independent realities or things. Rather, as form to matter, the soul is what gives the body its reality or "thingness."

62. People who are ill commonly resist the very thing that will make them better (see *On Order* 1.8.24).

63. The statement, as well as Augustine's strategy, is lifted from Cicero's *Hortensius* (frg. 36 [Müller]; see also *Tusculan Disputations* 5.10.28; Aristotle, *Nichomachean Ethics* 1.4; and Seneca, *On the Happy Life* 1.1). As Augustine puts it in the *City of God* 10.1: "It is the decided opinion of all who are capable of using their reason to some extent that all men wish to be happy" (see *Confessions* 10.20.29; *On the Trinity* 13.4.7).

64. See the *City of God* 8.8: "Who, then, but the most miserable will deny that whoever enjoys what he loves and loves the true and highest good is happy?"

65. *Gestiens*, translated here as "jumping for joy," refers literally to gesturing or throwing oneself about joyfully; figuratively it signifies being cheerful or eager.

66. For philosophy as a citadel, see *On Order* 1.11.32; for other uses of the metaphor of a citadel, see *Against the Academics* 1.9.24 and *Soliloquies* 1.10.17.

67. *Hortensius*, frg. 39 (Müller) (see Augustine, *On the Trinity* 13.5.8).

68. For a similar compliment, see *Confessions* 9.4.8.

69. See *On Order* for another testimony to the inspiration of Monica (2.1.1). The use of the word "flowed" suggests that the inspiration in question comes from the Holy Spirit (see 4.35 below; *On Order* 2.5.16, 2.9.26, and 2.19.51).

70. Given how they were defined in classical philosophy, happiness and misery are mutually exclusive. Hence in *Against the Academics* Augustine asserts that according to logic or dialectic "a man can't be both happy and miserable at the same time" (3.13.29).

71. That is, if I possess something, I should be able to retrieve it whenever I want.

72. See 4.26–28 below; see also *On Order* 2.18.48: "It is troublesome and perilous to become one with what can be separated."

73. On the relation between love and fear, see *Soliloquies* 1.9.16; see also *On Eighty-Three Different Questions* Q. 33: "No one doubts that the only cause for being afraid is either that we may lose what we love and have attained or that we may not attain what we love and have hoped for."

74. For more on "having" or "possessing" God or wisdom, see 3.19–21 below, *Against the Academics* 2.3.5; *Soliloquies* 1.1.3.

75. Adeodatus, Augustine's son (see 1.6 above).

76. For the importance of moderation in learning, see *On Order* 1.8.26 and 2.5.14.

77. See book one of *Against the Academics*, which took place immediately before *On the Happy Life*.

78. Literally, they made themselves erect. The three interlocutors who were present both here and at the discussion about the Academics were Licentius, Trygetius, and Navigius (see *Against the Academics* 1.1.4, 1.2.5).

79. See 2.10 above.

80. See Cicero, *Tusculan Disputations* 5.9.12ff; *On the Ends* 1.18.61, 5.29.86ff; Plotinus, *Enneads* 1.4.

81. *Viscera* can refer literally to the internal organs or metaphorically to one's innermost being, an ambivalence that Licentius here exploits.

82. Alypius, reluctantly perhaps, is on the side of the Academics (see *Against the Academics* 2.11.28–3.20.45), but he is currently away on a trip to Milan.

83. *Splen vitiosus*, literally, a defective or distempered spleen. The phrase is found in Columella, who uses it to describe a condition affecting swine (*On Agriculture* 7.10).

84. The illustrious person whom Navigius cites is Cicero. In the *Hortensius* Cicero mentions the sharp qualities of honey from Mount Hymettus near Athens (frg. 89 [Müller]). Hymettic honey is also mentioned in the description of a birthday cake by Tibullus (*Elegy* 1.7.53–54: "I shall honor you with incense / And I shall bring cakes sweetened with Mopsopian honey," Mopsopus being a mythical king of Attica, which includes Mount Hymettus). Navigius's description of Augustine's treat as tangled and prickly (*contortum et aculeatum*) is taken from *Academica* 2.24.75, where Cicero refers to "certain intricate and cunning sophisms" (*contorta et aculeata quaedam sophismata*). It is also an interesting coincidence to note that the Athenians stopped harvesting wild honey on or around November 13, Augustine's birthday (Pliny, *Natural History* 11.15.16).

85. See *Against the Academics* 1.2.5ff.

86. The word here for "succinct bit of reasoning" is *ratiuncula* (see *Against the Academics* 3.13.29, where it is translated "petty syllogism"; see also *Soliloquies* 1.15.29, 2.11.20). There may be a hint of irony in Augustine's use of the word, as Cicero generally uses the term pejoratively (see *Tusculan Disputations* 2.12.29, 4.19.43; *On the Nature of the Gods* 3.29.73).

87. The position he defended in *Against the Academics* 1.2.5ff.

88. For another reference to Augustine's coretreatants as banqueters, see *On Order* 2.1.1.

89. Augustine is addressing Manlius Theodorus (see 1.1 above). An *invitator*, translated here as summoner, was a slave who distributed invitations to a banquet (see Martial, *Epigram* 9.91.2).

90. The word Monica uses is *caducarius*, meaning one prone to falling or stumbling. Though *caducus* was a common medical term for someone with epilepsy or "the falling sickness," *caducarius* appears, judging by Augustine's qualification, to have been a North African colloquialism.

91. See 2.11–12 above.

92. Although ritual exorcisms were performed on advanced catechumens or *competentes* during the so-called Scrutinies as a part of their Lenten preparation for baptism, the reference to "rite" here is most likely the formulae that exorcists followed when driving demons out of an "energumen," a person possessed by a devil. These formulae were eventually written down and presented to exorcists in booklet form at their ordination (see Van Slyke, "The Order of Exorcist," 357–79).

93. For more on demons, see *Against the Academics* 1.7.20–21; *On Order* 2.9.27.

94. The "presiders"—literally, those who are in charge (*qui praesunt*)—were usually the bishop or a consecrated/ordained exorcist. Augustine may have in mind the incident in which St. Ambrose exorcised a boy named Pansopius through prayer and the imposition of hands (see Paulinus, *Life of Ambrose* 28.1–3). "Adjuring" in ecclesiastical Latin refers to commanding someone, usually a demon, in the name of God.

95. See 2.15 above.

96. See *On Order* 2.8.25; *Soliloquies* 2.20.36; *Confessions* 1.1.1.

97. Literally, what I had said in a twisted way by the necessity of the conclusion. Augustine is depicting himself as a passive agent who is compelled by the necessity of logic to arrive at this conclusion, but he is also hinting at the possibility that he may have deliberately employed twisted logic.

98. See 2.11 above.

99. See 2.16 above.

100. See 2.13–16 above.

101. See 2.14 above.

102. See 2.11 above.

103. There is a lacuna in the manuscript here, which Augustine, unable himself to correct decades later, notes in *Retractations* 1.2: "To be sure, I

discovered that this book has a gap in our copy and that it is missing no small amount, and in this condition it has been transcribed by certain brethren. And I had still not found an intact copy from which I could make emendations at the time that I was making these Retractations." Instead of the two words *aliquem beatum* (someone happy) after the lacuna, the β manuscript tradition has "who, according to you, also has someone happy there" (*qui pro te et ibi sic habet aliquem beatum*). The bracketed statements are my own conjectures. For more on what I suspect is the missing content, see "The Lacuna (3.22)" in the Commentary on *On the Happy Life*.

104. The passage is most likely from the lost sections of the *Hortensius*. Cicero makes a similar point in *The Paradoxes of the Stoics* 6.2.48.

105. See 1.6 above.

106. These two conclusions could be from the missing passage in 3.22, or they could be a reformulation of two things that were said in 2.11 above.

107. See 3.22 above.

108. See 2.11 above.

109. Augustine's line of argument here is drawn from the Stoics (see Arnim, *Stoicorum Veterum fragmenta* III, 151 frg. 572). Yet he later regrets this conclusion, for while it may be true in this life, it abstracts from our ultimate happiness at the end of time, when a new heaven and a new earth will be created:

> I do not like that I said . . . that in this lifetime the happy life dwells only in the soul of the wise man no matter what condition his body is in, seeing that the Apostle hopes for a perfect knowledge of God (that is, that than which nothing greater can be possessed by man) in the life to come. This alone should be called the happy life, where an incorruptible and immortal body will be subject to its spirit without any trouble or resistance. (*Retractations* 1.2)

110. Literally, a lack of these necessities can befall him (the wise man). Being free of bodily pain requires certain necessities that are ephemeral and capable of being taken away, what we refer to in the Commentary as unshareable goods (see "Misery and Need [4.24–29]").

111. See Terence, *Eunuch* 761. In the play, when the character Chremes wishes to avoid unnecessary trouble, he says, "*tu quod cavere possis, stultum admittere est.*" The only change that Augustine makes to the statement is to substitute *vitare* for *cavere*. While both verbs mean the same thing ("to avoid"), Augustine's substitution broadens the meaning

somewhat from potentially dangerous things to things in general—which are, Augustine implies, all potentially dangerous.

112. Terence, *Lady of Andros* 305; see Augustine, *On the Trinity* 13.7.10.

113. The wise man's acting according to virtue (*virtus*) and wisdom is an echo of 1 Cor 1:24, where Christ is called "the power (*virtus*) of God and the wisdom of God." The truly wise man, therefore, acts in Christ. See *Against the Academics* 2.1.1; also, see *On the Greatness of the Soul* 33.76; *On Eighty-Three Different Questions* Q. 26; *On the Teacher* 11.38. The divinity of "wisdom and true virtue (*virtus*)" are also mentioned in Plotinus, *Enneads* 4.7.10.

114. Literally, whatever their desire (*cupiditas*) asks for.

115. See 2.11 above.

116. See Cicero, *Hortensius* frg. 76 (Müller); *On Duties* 3.16.67. Sergius Orata was an affluent and powerful gourmand. Valerius Maximus mentions that in order to satisfy his palate, he had in his possession extraordinary contraptions for catching seafood delicacies and was a pioneer in oyster farming and the development of hypocausts, a central heating system for homes and baths that warmed a room by passing hot air through cavities under the floor and in the walls (*Memorable Deeds and Sayings* 9.1.1).

117. *Ingenium*, translated here and in the previous paragraph as "intelligence," refers to a natural capacity for thinking things through and for explaining, embellishing, and remembering (see Cicero, *On the Orator* 1.33.151, 2.35.147—51). It is translated elsewhere in this dialogue as "wits" or "intellectual aptitude" (see 1.6 above).

118. *Infidum hominem malo suo esse cordatum*, which can also mean, "The treacherous man is wise *in* his own evil." The proverb is of uncertain origin (see Sonny, "Neue Sprichtvörter," 487). One possibility is that it is somehow connected to Ennius's description of Aelius Sextus as recorded in Cicero's *On the Commonwealth* 1.18.30: "so wise (*cordatus*), and ever on his guard." In the dialogue, Laelius explains that Sextus was wise and cautious "not because he searched for what he could never find, but because he knew how to answer those who prayed to be rescued from worries and difficulties."

119. That is, Monica's position that misery is the same as need (see 4.23 above).

120. See 3.22 above, where Augustine quotes a passage in which Cicero argues that terms like "wealthy" and "poor" are as applicable to spiritual conditions as they are to financial. See also Socrates's prayer in Plato, *Phaedro* 279b–c: "May I consider the wise man to be rich."

121. For another testimony to Monica's godliness, see *On Order* 2.1.1.

122. In the *Tusculan Disputations* Cicero describes the soul of a wise man "always on guard in such a way that nothing unexpected, nothing unforeseen, nothing new in any way, can befall him" (4.17.37).

123. See Cicero, *On the Ends* 1.18.61: "No fool is happy and no wise man unhappy."

124. That is, Monica doubted (4.27).

125. See 4.23 above.

126. *Vitium* can also mean a defect or deficiency, with or without moral connotation (see *On Order* 1.3.8).

127. See 2.8 above.

128. *Esse et non esse:* literally, to be and not to be.

129. In Sallust's *Catiline*, Marcus Porcius Cato bewails the current state of Rome as one of "public need, private opulence" (52.22). Augustine's praise here of Sallust is echoed in the *City of God* 1.5, where Augustine refers to him as *nobilitate veritatis historicus*—a historian with nobility of truth. Aulus Gellius offers similar praise for Sallust's grammatical acumen in *Attic Nights* 17.1.3.

130. A friendly jab at Verecundus, the grammarian at whose villa they are staying.

131. Inspired intuitions of the mind* have an "oracular" value (see Cicero, *On Divination* 2.48.100).

132. Augustine's contrast of fullness and need, together with his mention of virtues or vices having a mother (here, and 2.8 above), are suggestive of the myth, told by Diotima and relayed by Socrates, about Penia (Poverty) and Poros (Resourcefulness) being the parents of Eros or Love (see Plato, *Symposium* 203a–e). Neoplatonists like Plotinus and Porphyry interpreted the father Poros in this myth as fullness or plenitude (see Plotinus, *Enneads* 3.5.6–10, esp. 9; Porphyry, *Thoughts Leading to the Intelligibles* 37–39).

133. Augustine expresses a similar sentiment to Nebridius in a letter that he wrote during his stay at Cassiciacum: "The philosophers placed 'wealth' in the category of intelligible things, 'need' in the category of sensible" (*Epistle* 3.2).

134. See Cicero, *Tusculan Disputations* 3.8.16. In his *Memorable Deeds and Sayings*, Valerius Maximus calls frugality the mother of good (bodily) health (2.5.6).

135. Cicero, *For King Deiotarus* 9.26.

136. See Aulus Gellius, *Attic Nights* 6.11.2: The ancients used the word " 'worthless' for a man of no importance or of no good fruit" (*nequam hominem nihili rei neque frugis bonae*).

137. See Cicero, *On Duties* 1.40.142. With extensive roots in both Cicero and Plotinus, *modus* (translated as "measure" or "limit," depending on context) is an important concept in the Cassiciacum dialogues (see 2.7 above and 4.34–35 below; *Against the Academics* 2.2.4, 2.3.9; *On Order* 1.8.26, 2.5.14, 2.19.50).

138. Etymologically, *affluentia* means "flowing to."

139. Some manuscripts have "and thus measure for the mind is in wisdom."

140. Terence, *Lady of Andros* 61; see also *On Order* 1.8.26. Augustine mentions a possible exception to this rule in *On Order* 2.20.52: "Loving such [divine] things with all one's might is perhaps always insufficient and, indeed, can never rightly be called excessive" (see also *Soliloquies* 1.13.22, 2.1.1).

141. See 4.23 above.

142. Fear, sorrow, and lust are three of the four "disturbances" (*perturbationes*) of the mind according to Cicero and the Stoics (see *On the Ends* 3.10.35; *Tusculan Disputations* 4.6.11). Augustine has replaced the fourth, joy, with *sordes*, baseness or illiberality, a fitting contrast to the generous fullness of authentic frugality.

143. The term in question is "hold oneself" (*se tenet*). See 3.18: "He is truly chaste who pays attention to God and holds himself to Him alone."

144. Literally, the deceitfulness of images (*simulacrorum fallacia*). In *Against the Academics* 3.6.13, Augustine likens the corporeal images that the senses grasp or help to form to the god Proteus, who changed into different shapes and appearances when captured (see also *On Order* 2.15.43). For more on the difference between the mind's grasp of the sensible and the intelligible, see *Soliloquies* 1.3.8–1.4.9; *On the Teacher* 12.29; *Confessions* 3.7.12, 7.1.2, 7.7.11, 10.8.12–10.12.19.

145. In *On Order* 2.11.31 Augustine speaks of the soul's "going forth" as a "fall down to mortal things"; in *Soliloquies* 1.1.3 he equates the soul's fall with its "turning away" from God; and in *On True Religion* 14.28 and 15.29, he argues that an act of the will has plunged the body into weakness and mortality. Although the image of the soul's fall or descent is common in philosophical literature (see Cato's remark in Cicero's *On Old Age* 21.77: "The celestial soul has been brought down from its most lofty home and buried, as it were, in the ground, a place contrary to its divine and eternal nature"), it is more often than not associated with Neoplatonic thought (see Plotinus, *Enneads* 4.8). For more references to the soul's falling or sinking in the Cassiciacum dialogues, see *Against the Academics* 3.15.34; *On Order* 2.17.45; *Soliloquies* 1.14.25.

146. See 1 Cor 1:24, 30.

147. See 2.11–12 above.

148. John 14:16. Wisdom and Truth, then, are identical to the Son of God, the Second Person of the Trinity. And Truth is also *intellectus*, the Divine Understanding or Intellect (see Plotinus, *Enneads* 5.5.1, 5.5.3).

149. That is, God the Father, the First Person of the Trinity (see *Against the Academics* 2.2.4; *On Order* 2.5.14; see also note 137 above on measure). Plotinus describes a Measure (*metron*) reigning above to which the measure in civic virtues bears a resemblance and which is "the Highest Good in the Supreme" (*Enneads* 1.2.2); he also describes the transcendent Good as "the Measure and Term of all" (*metron pantōn kai peras*) (*Enneads* 1.8.2). The Supreme Measure, then, is not merely the highest measurement but that by which all is measured and from which all measure is derived (see Plotinus, *Enneads* 5.5.4, which describes the One as "Measure unmeasured"). As such it is similar to Aristotle's notion of *telos* as the final cause or good for which all else exists or is done (see *Metaphysics* 994b9, 996a26; *Nicomachean Ethics* 1.1097a22). Other passages from Plotinus may have also influenced Augustine in this regard (see *Enneads* 1.8.4–6, 5.1.2, 5.1.6–7, 5.2.1, 5.5.1, 5.5.2, 5.5.11, 6.5.11).

150. Plotinus describes the One as a Measure that is not measured (see *Enneads* 5.5.4).

151. See Plotinus, *Enneads* 5.1.6, on the eternal generation of the Divine Mind from the One.

152. In the same way, the Son is never without the Father and vice versa (see *On Eighty-Three Different Questions* Q. 16; St. Ambrose, *Commentary on the Gospel According to St. Luke* 2.12; *On the Christian Faith* 1.8.55).

153. An *admonitio* is an act of reminding or a piece of advice. Augustine, following in the footsteps of Ambrose and Marius Victorinus, links divine *admonitio* with the Holy Spirit, the Third Person of the Trinity (see *Soliloquies* 1.1.2, 1.1.3, 1.13.23), or with inspiration in general (see *Against the Academics* 1.7.21). *Admonitio* is a Latin equivalent of the Greek *paraklēsis* (exhortation), from which the title Paraclete is derived (see John 14:16, etc.). Augustine here describes the procession of the Holy Spirit as a flowing or emanation (*emanare*); see *On Order* 2.5.16, 2.9.26, and 2.19.51, where similar language is used. The Supreme Measure or Font, then, is God the Father; the Truth, God the Son; and the Admonition emanating therefrom, God the Holy Spirit.

154. That is, our "inner eyes" or minds. Latin poets often used *lumen* as a reference to the human eye. For similar metaphors in Augustine's writing, see

On the Teacher 11.38; *On Genesis* 1.3.6; *Confessions* 7.10.16; *City of God* 10.2. For more on the eyes of the mind, see *Soliloquies* 1.6.12–1.7.14.

155. For the importance of having healthy eyes (of the mind), see *On Order* 2.4.11, 2.4.13, 2.19.51; *Soliloquies* 1.1.5, 2.6.12. Augustine uses the adverb *repente* here for "suddenly," the same word in the description of the first Pentecost in the Latin translations of Acts 2:2.

156. Augustine's image of being turned around (*conversus*) and beholding the whole is an echo of Plato's Allegory of the Cave (*Republic* 514a–516c). In the allegory, Socrates describes a prisoner's head being turned around from the shadows to the light, but he does not say who or what initiates the turning. Augustine seems to be implying that it is the Holy Spirit who begins our ascent outside the cave.

157. See *On Order* 2.5.16, which describes the Holy Spirit as emanating from God and suffering "no degeneration." Augustine makes these qualifications to distinguish the Holy Spirit from some of the emanations in Plotinus's philosophy that do suffer decay or are subordinate to the One.

158. That is, the Holy Spirit, who leads us to the Truth (see John 16:13); the Son of God, who is the Truth (see John 14:6); and God the Father, the Supreme Measure to whom we come or are united through His Son (John 14:6, Eph 2:18).

159. This verse is the concluding line of the hymn composed by St. Ambrose of Milan titled *Deus Creator Omnium* ("God, Creator of All Things," *Hymn* 2.32). The final stanza is:

> Let us petition Christ and the Father,
> And the Spirit of Christ and the Father;
> O mighty Unity through all things,
> O Trinity, cherish those who pray.

Deus Creator Omnium was to have a lasting impact on Augustine's imagination (see *Confessions* 2.6.12, 9.6.14, 9.12.32, 10.34.52, 11.27.35).

160. The theological virtues of faith, hope, and charity (1 Cor 13:13) are mentioned again in *Soliloquies* 1.6.13.

161. See 4.23 above.

162. *Quantas pro viribus possum.* A more literal rendering would be "with whatever strength I can [muster]," a possible allusion to Augustine's weakened physical condition at the time (see note 38 above).

163. *Hoc modo* can also mean "with this measure," hence Augustine's reply.

164. For the return to God, see 1.2 above (as homeland); *Against the Academics* 3.19.42 (also as homeland); *On Order* 1.7.20, 1.8.23; *Soliloquies* 1.1.2, 1.1.3,

1.1.6, 1.10.17, 1.11.18, 2.6.9. Augustine also speaks of returning to heaven as a metonymy for returning to God (*Against the Academics* 2.1.2, 2.9.22) and returning to the light (*On the Happy Life* 4.35; *Soliloquies* 1.6.13, 1.13.23, 2.19.33).

COMMENTARY

1. See *Against the Academics* 1.1.1, 3.2.2–4.
2. See Vitruvius, *Ten Books on Architecture* Pref. 1.
3. Diogenes, *Lives of Eminent Philosophers* 7.5.
4. See *Against the Academics* 3.18.41.
5. See *On Order* 1.11.31.
6. See *Against the Academics* 3.14.30.
7. See *Soliloquies* 1.13.22.
8. Later in the dialogue, Augustine characterizes bodily necessities as (unshareable) goods that "are susceptible to becoming scarce" (4.25).
9. See Plutarch, *Life of Alexander* 7.3–4.
10. Augustine himself benefited from such haughty guides. In the *Confessions*, he is directed to the books of the Platonists, which would have a profound effect on him, by "an incredibly conceited man" (7.9.13). Moreover, both the imagery and the content of *Confessions* 7.20.26 and 27 have strong parallels to this section of *On the Happy Life*.
11. Augustine, *On the Nature and Origin of the Soul* 1.10.12.
12. See Homer, *Odyssey* 13.65–128.
13. See *Odyssey* 11.119–23.
14. See *Odyssey* 5.84–86, 151.
15. See *Odyssey* 9.85–102.
16. See *Odyssey* 10.149–597.
17. See *Odyssey* 12.37–208.
18. *Enneads* 1.6.8.
19. See *Confessions* 6.3.3–4.
20. See *Retractations* 1.2.
21. We do not know whether Theodorus ever obliged Augustine's request.
22. Navigius, for instance, is able to cite two Ciceronian passages in *On the Happy Life* 2.14.
23. See *On Order* 1.11.31.
24. See *On Order* 1.8.24.
25. See *Against the Academics* 3.19.42.
26. See *On Order* 1.11.31.

27. Porphyry, *Life of Plotinus* 1.
28. *Life of Plotinus* 2.
29. See *Against the Academics* 1.1.3, 1.2.5, 1.4.11.
30. See *Against the Academics* 2.4.10 and 3.4.7.
31. See the Time Line.
32. See the Translation Key.
33. See *On Order* 1.8.25, where Augustine contrasts knowing and unknowing creatures (*scientia et nescientia*).
34. See Argetsinger, "Birthday Rituals."
35. Chronologically, books two and three of *Against the Academics* and all of *On Order* take place after *On the Happy Life*. Tensions are particularly obvious in *On Order*.
36. Fortin, "Augustine and the Problem of Human Goodness," 28.
37. Fortin, "Augustine and the Problem of Human Goodness," 29.
38. *On the Ends* 3.14.48.
39. "That is the reason for the strange melancholy often haunting inhabitants of democracies in the midst of abundance, and of that disgust with life sometimes gripping them in calm and easy circumstances" (Tocqueville, *Democracy*, vol. 2, pt. II, ch. 13, 538).
40. See *Soliloquies* 1.4.9, 1.7.13–14, 2.15.27.
41. See *Soliloquies* 1.4.9–10.
42. See *Against the Academics* 1.2.5.
43. See *Soliloquies* 1.1.6; see also *Against the Academics* 3.12.27.
44. *Epistle* 118.3.13.
45. See *Confessions* 7.10.16.
46. See Aristotle, *Nicomachean Ethics* 9.8 (1168a30–1169b1).
47. See "Eudaimonism" in the Introduction to *On the Happy Life*.
48. See *Confessions* 9.6.14: "But You took him early from this earth, and I think of him utterly without anxiety, for there is nothing in his boyhood or youth or anywhere in him to cause me to fear."
49. See *On the Happy Life* 1.4, where a similar phrase is translated "hold my head up higher," and *On Order* 1.1.1, at the translation, "heads held high."
50. See book one of *Against the Academics*.
51. See books two and three of *Against the Academics*.
52. See *On Agriculture* 7.10.
53. See Celsus, *On Medicine* 4.16. For a swollen spleen, "all sweets are harmful, as are milk and cheese; sour things, on the other hand, are especially suitable."

54. Augustine has no difficulty admitting that he is an unhappy fool (see *Against the Academics* 3.5.12, 3.20.43), but the group may not yet feel the same way.

55. See Aristotle, *Nicomachean Ethics* 8.7 (1158b10–30).

56. See *On Order* 1.4.10.

57. See Leake, "Lesser Hippias," 293.

58. See *Against the Academics* 3.16.35.

59. *Banquet of the Learned* 1.13 (7e).

60. See *Confessions* 9.11.27, where Navigius, "savouring of earthly things," worries about the location of Monica's grave.

61. See *On the Happy Life* 3.19.

62. *Confessions* 1.4.4.

63. See *Retractations* 1.2.

64. See Foley, "Recovering the Lost Passages."

65. See "The Threefold End" in the General Introduction.

66. See *On the Trinity* 9.11.16; see also *On the Immortality of the Soul* 8.13.

67. See *On Order* 2.3.10.

68. See *On Order* 2.3.10; *Soliloquies* 1.13.23.

69. See *Confessions* 7.13.19.

70. See *Confessions* 7.13.19.

71. See *On the Happy Life* 4.29–31 (worthlessness, neediness, darkness, and nakedness); *On Order* 2.3.8–10 (folly) and 2.8.22–23 (evil); *Soliloquies* 2.9.16 (falsehood) and 2.17.31 (emptiness). See also *On the Teacher* 2.3 (nothingness); *On True Religion* 19.37 (vice); *Confessions* 7.13.19 (evil), 10.16.24 (forgetfulness).

72. See *Symposium* 202b, *Republic* 4.430b–431c.

73. A heuristic is something that is instrumental in finding (*euriskein*); often, it is a method or series of clues for discovering the solution to a problem. Augustine has a penchant for heuristic definitions at Cassiciacum (see *Against the Academics* 1.2.5; *On Order* 1.9.27). For more heuristic definitions in the Cassiciacum dialogues, see "Setting the Stage (1.2.5–6)" in the Commentary on *Against the Academics*.

74. See Kenyon, *Augustine*, 94. For the Academic skeptics' theory of probability, see *Against the Academics* 2.5.12ff.

75. See *Confessions* 6.3.4.

76. See *Confessions* 7.1.2: The mental act, which is "something, and something great," forms all images yet is itself not a bodily image.

77. See *Against the Academics* 3.19.42; *On Order* 2.5.16.

78. See *Confessions* 7.10.16.

79. See Kenyon, *Augustine*, 92–95.

80. See Plotinus, *Enneads* 6.6.7.

81. If my hypothesis about the lacuna in 3.22 is correct, the same bitter truth that is revealed here was revealed there as well, namely, that the person who seeks God but does not "have" him is miserable. The difference, however, is that in the missing passage Augustine probably did not indict himself and the others by stating explicitly that "*we* are . . . not yet wise and happy" as he does here in 4.35.

82. This is an arresting statement, for Augustine does not explicitly state that happiness is knowing the Father and the Son and the Holy Spirit; rather, he states that happiness is knowing the Holy Spirit, who stands in such and such a relation to the Father and the Son. True, the need to know the entire Trinity for the sake of happiness is strongly implied, but the focus on the Holy Spirit is chronological or in accordance with the economical missions of the divine persons: our happiness begins with a visit from the Holy Spirit, so to speak. Augustine thus steers clear of a heresy of subordinationism.

83. Matt 26:26; see also Mark 14:24 and Luke 22:20.

84. See Athenaeus, *Banquet of the Learned* 15.49 (694b).

85. See the collect for the fifth Sunday after Pentecost in the 1962 *Missale Romanum*, which serves as an apt summary of *On the Happy Life*: "O God, who hast prepared for those who love Thee such good things as eye hath not seen; pour into our hearts such love towards Thee, that loving Thee in all things and above all things, we may obtain Thy promises, which exceed all that we can desire."

86. See Ohlmann, *De Sancti Augustini dialogis*, 17–27; O'Donnell, *Augustine Confessions* 3:86.

87. *Confessions* 10.23.33.

88. For a survey of the scholarship, see O'Donnell, *Augustine Confessions* 3:86.

89. See *Confessions* 10.6.9: "But what is it that I love when I love You? Not the beauty of any bodily thing, nor the order of seasons, not the brightness of light that rejoices the eye, nor the sweet melodies of all songs, nor the sweet fragrance of flowers and ointments and spices: not manna nor honey, not the limbs that carnal love embraces. None of these things do I love in loving my God. Yet in a sense I do love light and melody and fragrance and food and embrace when I love my God—the light and the voice and the fragrance and the food and embrace in the soul, when that light shines upon my soul which no place can contain, that voice sounds which no time can take from me, I breathe that fragrance which no wind scatters, I eat the food which is not lessened by eating, and I lie in the embrace which satiety never comes to sunder. This it is that I love, when I love my God."

BIBLIOGRAPHY

All translations are the author's unless otherwise noted.

Aeschylus. *Oresteia (Agamemnon, The Libation Bearers,* and *The Eumenides).*

Alfaric, Prosper. *L'évolution intellectuelle de saint Augustin.* Paris: Émile Nourry, 1918.

Allen, James. "Academic Probabilism and Stoic Epistemology." *Classical Quarterly* 44 (1994): 85–113.

Ambrose of Milan. *Commentary on the Gospel According to St. Luke (Expositio in Lucam).*

———. *Exposition of Psalm 118 (Explanatio psalmorum CXVIII).*

———. *Exposition of Twelve Psalms (Explanatio psalmorum XII).*

———. *Hymns (Hymni).*

———. *On Isaac (De Isaac).*

———. *On Jacob and the Happy Life (De Jacob et vita beata).*

———. *On Naboth (De Nabuthae).*

———. *On the Christian Faith (De fide).*

———. *On the Good of Death (De bono mortis).*

———. *On the Mysteries (De mysteriis).*

———. *On the Passing of His Brother Satyrus (De excessu fratris).*

———. *On the Sacraments (De sacramentis).*

———. *On Virgins (De virginibus).*

Ambrosiaster. *Questions on the Old and New Testament (Quaestiones Veteris et Novi Testamenti).*

Apuleius. *On Plato and His Doctrine (De dogmate Platonis).*

Argetsinger, Kathryn. "Birthday Rituals: Friends and Patrons in Roman Poetry and Cult." *Classical Antiquity* 11, no. 2 (October 1992): 175–93.

Aristotle. *Aristotle's Metaphysics*. Translated by Hippocrates G. Apostle. Bloomington: Indiana University Press, 1966.

——. *Categories*.

——. *History of Animals*.

——. *Nicomachean Ethics*. Translations from *Nicomachean Ethics*. Translated by Martin Ostwald. Upper Saddle River, NJ: Prentice Hall, 1999.

——. *On the Soul*.

——. *Physics*. Translations from *Physics, Volume I: Books 1–4*. Translated by P. H. Wicksteed. Cambridge, MA: Harvard University Press, 1957.

——. *Poetics*.

——. *Posterior Analytics*.

Arnim, Hans Friedrich August von. *Stoicorum Veterum fragmenta*. Stuttgart: B. G. Teubner, 1964.

Arrian. *Discourses of Epictetus* (*Epiktētou Diatribai*).

Asiedu, F. "The Wise Man and the Limits of Virtue in *De Beata Vita*: Stoic Self-Sufficiency or Augustinian Irony?" *Augustiniana* 49 (1999): 215–34.

Athenaeus. *The Banquet of the Learned* (*Deipnosophistae*).

Augustine of Hippo. *Against Cresconius* (*Contra Cresconium*).

——. *Against Faustus* (*Contra Faustum*).

——. *Against Fortunatus the Manichaean* (*Contra Fortunatum*).

——. *Against Julian* (*Contra Julianum*).

——. *Against Lying* (*Contra Mendacium*).

——. *Against the Academics* (*Contra Academicos*). Translation based on *Contra academicos, De beata vita, De ordine, De magistro, De libero arbitrio*. Edited by W. M. Green and K. D. Daur. Volume 29 of *Corpus Christianorum, Series Latina*. Turnhout: Brepols, 1970.

——. *Confessions* (*Confessiones*). Translations from *The Confessions of Saint Augustine*. Translated by F. J. Sheed and edited by Michael P. Foley. 2nd ed. Indianapolis, IN: Hackett, 2006.

——. *City of God* (*De civitate Dei*).

——. *Enchiridion*.

——. *Epistles* (*Epistulae*).

——. *Explanations of the Psalms* (*Enarrationes in psalmos*).

——. *The Literal Meaning of Genesis* (*De Genesi ad litteram*).

——. *On Christian Doctrine* (*De doctrina Christiana*).

——. *On Dialectic* (*De dialectica*).

——. *On Eighty-Three Different Questions* (*De diversis quaestionibus LXXXIII*).

——. *On Free Choice of the Will* (*De libero arbitrio*).

——. *On Genesis Against the Manichaeans* (*De Genesi adversus Manicheos*).

——. *On Heresies* (*De haeresibus*).

——. *On Lying* (*De mendacio*).

——. *On Music* (*De musica*).

——. *On Order* (*De ordine*). Translation based on *Contra academicos, De beata vita, De ordine, De magistro, De libero arbitrio*. Edited by W. M. Green and K. D. Daur. Volume 29 of *Corpus Christianorum, Series Latina*. Turnhout: Brepols, 1970.

——. *On the Happy Life* (*De beata vita*). Translation based on *Contra academicos, De beata vita, De ordine, De magistro, De libero arbitrio*. Edited by W. M. Green and K. D. Daur. Volume 29 of *Corpus Christianorum, Series Latina*. Turnhout: Brepols, 1970.

——. *On the Greatness of the Soul* (*De quantitate animae*).

——. *On the Immortality of the Soul* (*De immortalitate animae*).

——. *On the Morals of the Catholic Church* (*De moribus ecclesiae*).

——. *On the Nature and Origin of the Soul* (*De natura et origine animae*).

——. *On the Teacher* (*De magistro*).

——. *On the Trinity* (*De Trinitate*).

——. *On the Usefulness of Believing* (*De utilitate credendi*).

——. *On the Work of Monks* (*De opere monachorum*).

——. *On True Religion* (*De vera religione*).

——. *Questions on the Heptateuch* (*Quaestiones in Heptateuchum*).

——. *Retractations* (*Retractationes*).

——. *Sermons* (*Sermones*).

——. *Soliloquies* (*Soliloquia*). Translation based on *Soliloquia, De inmortalitate animae, De quantitate animae*. Edited by Wolfgang Hörmann. Volume 89 of *Corpus Scriptorum Ecclesiasticorum Latinorum*. Vienna: Hoelder-Pichler-Tempsky, 1986.

Aurelianus, Caelius. *Tardae*.

Ayres, Lewis. " 'Giving Wings to Nicaea': Reconceiving Augustine's Earliest Trinitarian Theology." *Augustinian Studies* 38, no. 1 (2007): 21–40.

Bagley, Paul. "On the Practice of Esotericism." *Journal of the History of Ideas* 53, no. 2 (April–June 1992): 231–47.

Barish, Jonas. *The Antitheatrical Prejudice*. Berkeley: University of California Press, 1981.

Beatrice, Pier Franco. "Quosdam Platonicorum Libros: The Platonic Readings of Augustine in Milan." *Vigiliae Christianae* 43 (1989): 248–81.

Berger, Adolf. *Encyclopedic Dictionary of Roman Law*. Philadelphia: American Philosophical Society, 1953.

Bermon, Emmanuel. " '*Contra Academicos vel De Academicis*' (*Retract.* I, 1): Saint Augustin et les *Academica* de Cicéron." *Revue des Études Anciennes* 111, no. 1 (2009): 75–93.

Bett, Richard. "Carneades' Distinction Between Assent and Approval." *Monist* 73, no. 1 (1990): 3–20.

Bezancon, J. N. "Le mal et l'existence temporelle chez Plotin et S. Augustin." *Revue des Études Augustiniennes* 3 (1965): 133–60.

Bickerton, Derek. "Modes of Interior Monologue: A Formal Definition." *Modern Language Quarterly* 28, no. 2 (1967): 229–39.

Boersma, Gerald P. *Augustine's Early Theology of Image.* Oxford: Oxford University Press, 2016.

Boethius. *First Edition of the Commentary on Porphyry's Isagoge* (*In Porphyrii Isagogen commentorum editio prima*).

Bogan, Mary Inez. *The Vocabulary and Style of the Soliloquies and Dialogues of St. Augustine.* Washington, DC: Catholic University of America Press, 1935.

Boissier, Gaston. "La conversion de saint Augustin." *Revue des Deux Mondes* 85 (1888): 43–69.

Bolyard, Charles. "Augustine, Epicurus, and External World Skepticism." *Journal of the History of Philosophy* 44, no. 2 (2006): 157–68.

Boone, Mark J. *The Conversion and Therapy of Desire: Augustine's Theology of Desire in the Cassiciacum Dialogues.* Eugene, OR: Pickwick, 2016.

———. "The Role of Platonism in Augustine's 386 Conversion to Christianity." *Religion Compass* 9, no. 5 (May 2015): 151–61.

Bourke, Vernon J. "Joy in Augustine's Ethics." *Saint Augustine Lecture Series* (1978): 9–55.

Bowerman, Helen C. "The Birthday as a Commonplace of Roman Elegy." *Classical Journal* 12, no. 5 (February 1917): 310–18.

Boyer, Charles. *Christianisme et Néo-Platonisme dans la formation de saint Augustin.* 2nd ed. Rome: Catholic Book Agency, 1953.

Brittain, Charles, trans. *On Academic Scepticism.* Indianapolis, IN: Hackett, 2006.

Brown, Peter. *Augustine of Hippo.* Berkeley: University of California Press, 2000.

Brown, Ruth Allison, trans. *S. Aureli Augustini de Beata Vita.* Washington, DC: Catholic University of America Press, 1944.

Burns, J. Patout. "Ambrose Preaching to Augustine: The Shaping of Faith." In *Augustine: Second Founder of the Faith. Collectanea Augustiniana* 1, edited by J. Schnaubelt and Frederick Van Fleteren, 373–86. New York: Peter Lang, 1990.

Burton, Philip. "The Vocabulary of the Liberal Arts in Augustine's *Confessions.*" In *Augustine and the Disciplines: From Cassiciacum to* Confessions, edited by Karla Pollman and Mark Vessey, 141–64. Oxford: Oxford University Press (2007).

Cairns, Francis. "Horace Odes 3.17 and the Genre Genethliakon." In *Roman Lyric: Collected Papers on Catullus and Horace*, 412–40. Berlin: de Gruyter, 2012.

———. "Propertius 3,10 and Roman Birthdays." *Hermes* 99 (1971): 149–55.

Capella, Martianus. *On the Marriage of Philology and Mercury (De nuptiis).*

Cary, Phillip. *Augustine's Invention of the Inner Self: The Legacy of a Christian Platonist.* Oxford: Oxford University Press, 2000.

———. "What Licentius Learned: A Narrative Reading of the Cassiciacum Dialogues." *Augustinian Studies* 29, no. 1 (1998): 141–63.

Catapano, Giovanni. "Augustine's Treatise *De Immortalitate Animae* and the Proof of the Soul's Immortality in *Soliloquia.*" *Documenti e studi sulla tradizione filosofica medieval* 25 (2014): 67–84.

———, trans. *Aurelio Agostino, Tutti i dialoghi.* Milan: Bompiani, 2006.

———. "In philosophiae gremium confugere: Augustine's View of Philosophy in the First Book of the *Contra Academicos.*" Dionysius 18 (2000): 46–68.

Celsus. *The True Word (Logos Alethes).*

Celsus, Cornelius. *On Medicine (De medicina).*

Censorinus. *The Birthday Book (De die natali)*

Charalabopoulos, Nikos. *Platonic Drama and Its Ancient Reception.* Cambridge: Cambridge University Press, 2012.

Chesterton, G. K. *Orthodoxy.* San Francisco: Ignatius Press, 1997. First published 1908.

Cicero, Marcus Tullius. *Academica.*

———. *Against Verres (In Verrem).*

———. *Against Verres II (In Verrem II).*

———. *Brutus.*

———. *Consolation (Consolatio).* Numbering of fragments from *M. Tulli Ciceronis Consolationis Fragmenta.* Edited by Claudius Vitelli. Florence: Arnaldo Mondadori Editore, 1979.

———. *For Aulus Caecina (Pro Caecina).*

———. *For Flaccus (Pro Flacco).*

———. *For King Deiotarus (Pro rege Deiotaro).*

———. *For Lucius Murena (Pro Murena).*

———. *For Rabirius (Pro C. Rabirio).*

———. *For Roscius the Comedian (Pro Roscio comoedo).*

———. *For Sextus Roscius of Ameria* (*Pro Sexto Roscio Amerino*).

———. *Hortensius* (*Hortensius*).

———. *Letters to Atticus* (*Epistulae ad Atticum*).

———. *Letters to Family Friends* (*Epistulae ad Familiares*).

———. *Letters to Quintus His Brother* (*Epistulae ad Quintum Fratrem*).

———. *On Divination* (*De divinatione*).

———. *On Duties* (*De officiis*).

———. *On Fate* (*De fato*).

———. *On Friendship* (*De amicitia*).

———. *On Old Age* (*Cato Major de Senectute*)

———. *On Oratorical Classification* (*De partitione oratoria*).

———. *On Rhetorical Invention* (*De inventione*).

———. *On the Commonwealth* (*De re publica*). Numbering of fragments from *Cicerón. La République*. 2 vols. Edited by Esther Bréguet. Paris: Les Belles Lettres, 1980.

———. *On the Ends of Good and Evil Things* (*De finibus bonorum et malorum*).

———. *On the Laws* (*De legibus*).

———. *On the Nature of the Gods* (*De natura deorum*).

———. *On the Orator* (*De oratore*).

———. *The Orator* (*Orator*).

———. *The Paradoxes of the Stoics* (*Paradoxa Stoicorum*).

———. *Topics* (*Topica*).

———. *Tusculan Disputations* (*Disputationes Tusculanae*).

Coleridge, Samuel Taylor. "Aids to Reflection." In *The Complete Works of Samuel Taylor Coleridge*, Volume 1. Edited by W. G. T. Shedd. New York: Harper, 1884.

Columella. *On Agriculture* (*De re rustica*).

Consolmagno, Guy. "The Virtuous Astronomer: How Studying the Stars Is Shaped by Faith, Hope, and Love." Unpublished paper presented at Baylor University's Institute for Faith and Learning, March 2, 2010.

Conybeare, Catherine. "The Duty of a Teacher: Liminality and *disciplina* in Augustine's *De Ordine*." In *Augustine and the Disciplines: From Cassiciacum to Confessions*, edited by Karla Pollman and Mark Vessey, 49–65. Oxford: Oxford University Press, 2007.

———. *The Irrational Augustine*. Oxford: Oxford University Press, 2006.

Cooper, Stephen A. "Scripture at Cassicacum: I Corinthians 13:13 in the *Soliloquies*." *Augustinian Studies* 27, no. 2 (1996): 21–46.

Courcelle, Pierre. "Les premières confessions de saint Augustin." *Revue des Études Latines* 22 (1945): 155–74.

———. "Litiges sur la lecture des 'libri Platonicorum' par saint Augustin." *Augustiniana* 4 (1954): 225–39.

———. *Recherches sur les Confessions.* Paris: E. de Boccard, 1950.

Crosson, Frederick J. "Cicero and Augustine." Unpublished lecture, 1994 Bradley Lecture, Boston College.

———. "Esoteric Versus Latent Teaching." *Review of Metaphysics* 59, no. 1 (September 2005): 73–93.

Curley, Augustine J. *Augustine's Critique of Skepticism: A Study of* Contra Academicos. New York: Peter Lang, 1997.

Cyprian of Carthage. *On the Lord's Prayer* (*De dominica oratione*).

D'Arms, John H. "Slaves at Roman Convivia." In *Dining in a Classical Context,* edited by William Slater, 171–84. Ann Arbor: University of Michigan Press, 1991.

Dennis, Phillip W. "The Three Augustines of *Contra Academicos.*" Agkyra. com, 1–26 (December 2007). https://www.academia.edu/22987961/The _Three_Augustines_of_Contra_Academicos.

Descartes, René. *Discourse on Method.* Translated by Donald A. Cress. 3rd ed. Indianapolis, IN: Hackett, 1998.

Diggs, Bernard J. "St. Augustine Against the Academicians." *Traditio* 7 (1949–1951): 73–93.

Dillon, John M., and A. A. Long, eds. *The Question of "Eclecticism": Studies in Later Greek Philosophy.* Berkeley: University of California Press, 1988.

Di Lorenzo, Raymond. "Ciceronianism and Augustine's Conception of Philosophy." *Augustinian Studies* 13 (1982): 171–76.

Diomedes the Grammarian. *Grammar* (*Ars Grammatica*).

Dix, T. Keith. "Vergil in the Grynean Grove: Two Riddles in the Third Eclogue." *Classical Philology* 90, no. 3 (July 1995): 256–62.

Djuth, Marianne. "Augustine, Monica, and the Love of Wisdom." *Augustinian Studies* 39, no. 2 (2008): 237–52.

———. "Philosophy in a Time of Exile: Vera Philosophia and the Incarnation." *Augustinian Studies* 38, no. 1 (2007): 281–300.

Dobell, Brian. *Augustine's Intellectual Conversion: The Journey from Platonism to Christianity.* Cambridge: Cambridge University Press, 2009.

Doignon, Jean, trans. "Développements stoïcisants d'Augustin autour de l' 'exemplum' cicéronien d'Orata." In *Signum Pietatis,* 53–61. Würzburg: Augustinus-Verlag, 1989.

———. *Dialogues philosophiques: La vie heureuse* 4/1. Paris: Institut d'Études Augustiniennes, 1986.

——. *Dialogues philosophiques: L'ordre* 4/2. Paris: Institut d'Études Augustiniennes, 1997.

——. "La *praxis* de l'*admonitio* dans les Dialogues de Cassiciacum de saint Augustin." *Vetera Christiana* 23 (1986): 21–37.

Donahue, John F. "Toward a Typology of Roman Public Feasting." *American Journal of Philology* 124, no. 3 (Autumn 2003): 423–41.

Doucet, Dominique. "Augustin, *Confessions*, 4, 16, 28–29, *Soliloques* 2, 20, 34–36, et les *Commentaires des Catégories*." *Rivista di Filosofia Neo-scolastica* (2001): 372–92.

——. "Être dans un sujet: Sol. II, 12, 22." *Augustiniana* 43 (1993): 43–51.

——. "La problématique de la lumière chez Augustin." *Bulletin de Littérature Ecclésiastique* 100, no. 1 (1999): 31–58.

——. "L'époux des âmes. Porphyre, Ambroise, et Augustin, *De bono mortis* 14 20; *De ordine* I, 8, 24." *Revue des Études Augustiniennes* 41 (1995): 231–52.

——. "Le thème du médecin dans les premiers dialogues philosophiques de saint Augustin." *Augustiniana* 39 (1989): 447–61.

——. "Similitudo mater ueritatis, dissimilitudo mater falsitatis." *Archives de Philosophie* 61 (1998): 269–91.

——. "Sol. I, 1, 2–6: Recherche de Dieu, incarnation et philosophie." *Revue des Études Augustiniennes* 36 (1990): 91–119.

——. "Sol. I, 14, 24–15, 30, et le médecin complaisant." *Revue des Sciences religieuses* 247–48 (1991): 33–50.

——. "Sol. II, 13, 23, et les magni philosophi." *Revue des Études Augustiniennes* 39 (1993): 109–28.

——. "Sol. II, 18, 32: La vérité, le vrai et la forme du corps." *Revue des sciences philosophiques et théologiques* 77 (1993): 547–66.

——. "Speculum cogitationis: Sol. II, 20, 35." *Revue de Philosophie Ancienne* 10, no. 2 (1992): 221–45.

Douglass, Laurie. "Voice Re-Cast: Augustine's Use of Conversation in De ordine and the Confessions." *Augustinian Studies* 27, no. 1 (1996): 39–54.

Downey, Patrick. *Desperately Wicked: Philosophy, Christianity, and the Human Heart.* Downers Grove, IL: IVP Academic, 2009.

——. *Serious Comedy: The Philosophical and Theological Significance of Tragic and Comic Writing in the Western Tradition.* Lanham, MD: Lexington Books, 2001.

Dox, Donnalee. *The Idea of the Theater in Latin Christian Thought: Augustine to the Fourteenth Century.* Ann Arbor: University of Michigan Press, 2004.

Dutton, Blake D. *Augustine and Academic Skepticism: A Philosophical Study.* Ithaca, NY: Cornell University Press, 2016.

Elsner, Jaś. "Caught in the Ocular: Visualising Narcissus in the Roman World." In *Echoes of Narcissus*, edited by Lieve Spaas, 89–110. New York: Berghahn, 2000.

Ennius. *The Annals (Annales)*.

Euripides. *Bacchae*.

Eusebius of Caesaria. *Preparation for the Gospel (Praeparatio evangelica)*.

Faas, Patrick. *Around the Roman Table: Food and Feasting in Ancient Rome*. Translated by Shaun Whiteside. New York: Palgrave Macmillan, 1994.

Ferrari, Leo C. *The Conversions of Saint Augustine*. Villanova, PA: Villanova University Press, 1984.

Festugière, A. J. *Personal Religion Among the Greeks*. Berkeley, CA: University of California Press, 1954.

Fitzgerald, Allan D., ed. *Augustine Through the Ages*. Grand Rapids: Eerdmans, 1999.

Flaccus, Varrius. *The Lexicon of Festus (De Verborum Signficatu)*.

Flint, Thomas, ed. *Christian Philosophy*. Notre Dame: University of Notre Dame Press, 1990.

Foley, Michael P. "Cicero, Augustine, and the Philosophical Roots of the Cassiciacum Dialogues." *Revue des Études Augustiniennes* 45, no. 1 (1999): 51–77.

———. "The Other Happy Life: The Political Dimension to St. Augustine's Cassiciacum Dialogues." *Review of Politics* 65, no. 2 (Spring 2003): 165–83.

———. "Recovering the Lost Passages of St. Augustine's *On the Happy Life (De beata vita)*." Forthcoming.

———. "A Spectacle to the World: The Theatrical Meaning of Saint Augustine's *Soliloquies*." *Journal of Early Christian Studies* 22, no. 2 (Summer 2014): 243–60.

Fortin, Ernest L. "Augustine and the Hermeneutics of Love: Some Preliminary Considerations." In Fortin, *Birth of Philosophic Christianity*, 1–19.

———. "Augustine and the Problem of Human Goodness." In Fortin, *Birth of Philosophic Christianity*," 21–39.

———. *The Birth of Philosophic Christianity: Studies in Early Christian and Medieval Thought*. Volume 1 of *Ernest L. Fortin: Collected Essays*. Edited by J. Brian Benestad. Lanham, MD: Rowman & Littlefield, 1996.

———. *Ever Ancient, Ever New: Ruminations on the City, the Soul, and the Church*. Volume 4 of *Ernest L. Fortin: Collected Essays*. Edited by Michael P. Foley. Lanham, MD: Rowman & Littlefield, 2007.

———. Foreword to *Augustine's* Contra Academicos: *A Study* by Augustine J. Curley, ix–xi. New York: Peter Lang, 1996.

——. "The Nature of the Christian Message." In Fortin, *Ever Ancient*, 31–45.

——. "The Patristic Sense of Community." In Fortin, *Birth of Philosophic Christianity*, 61–77.

——. "Reflections on the Proper Way to Read Augustine the Theologian." In Fortin, *Birth of Philosophic Christianity*, 95–114.

——. Review of *Saint Augustine's Early Theory of Man, A.D. 386–391*, by Robert J. O'Connell. In Fortin, *Birth of Philosophic Christianity*, 309–11.

——. "The 'Rhetoric' of the Church Fathers." In Fortin, *Ever Ancient*, 47–58.

——. "The *Viri Novi* of Arnobius." In Fortin, *Birth of Philosophic Christianity*, 169–96.

Frank, Tenney. *Life and Literature in the Roman Republic*. Berkeley: University of California Press, 1965.

Frede, Michael. "Stoic Epistemology." In *The Cambridge History of Hellenistic Philosophy*, edited by Keimpe Algra, Jonathan Barnes, Jaap Mansfield, and Malcolm Schofield, 295–322. Cambridge: Cambridge University Press, 1999.

Fredrekson, Paula. "Paul and Augustine: Conversion Narratives, Orthodox Tradition, and the Retrospective Self." *Journal of Theological Studies* 37, no. 1 (April 1986): 3–34.

Funaioli, H. *Grammaticae Romanae fragmenta*. Leipzig: Teubner, 1907.

Garvey, Mary Patricia, trans. *Saint Augustine: Against the Academics*. Milwaukee: Marquette University Press, 1957.

Gellius, Aulus. *Attic Nights (Noctes Atticae)*.

Gerson, Lloyd, ed. *Cambridge Companion to Plotinus*. Cambridge: Cambridge University Press, 1996.

Gilligan, Thomas F., trans. *The Soliloquies of St. Augustine*. New York: Cosmopolitan Science and Art Service, 1943.

Gilson, Étienne. *Introduction à l'étude de saint Augustin*. Paris: Vrin, 1929.

Girard, René. *I See Satan Fall like Lightning*. Translated by James G. Williams. Ossining, NY: Orbis, 2001.

——. *Violence and the Sacred*. Translated by Patrick Gregory. New York: W. W. Norton, 1972.

Goldhill, Simon, ed. *The End of Dialogue in Antiquity*. Oxford: Oxford University Press, 2008.

Gregory of Nazianzus. *Oration 43: Panegyric on St. Basil*.

Grilli, Albertus. *Hortensius*. Milan: Istituto Editoriale Cisalpino, 1962.

Hadot, Ilsetraut. *Arts libéraux et philosophie dans la pensée antique*. 2nd ed. Paris: Vrin, 2005.

Hadot, Pierre. *What Is Ancient Philosophy?* Translated by Michael Chase. Cambridge, MA: Belknap, 2004.

Hagendahl, Harald. *Augustine and the Latin Classics.* 2 vols. Gothenburg: Göteborg, 1967, quoted in Bennett, Camille. "The Conversion of Vergil: The *Aeneid* in Augustine's *Confessions.*" *Revue des Études Augustiniennes,* 34 (1988): 47–69.

Halliburton, R. J. "The Inclination to Retirement: The Retreat of Cassiciacum and the 'Monastery' of Tagaste." *Texte und Untersuchungen zur Geschichte der Altchristlichen Literatur,* Band 80, 329–40. Berlin: Akademie, 1962.

Halliwell, Stephen. *The Aesthetics of Mimesis: Ancient Texts and Modern Traditions.* Princeton: Princeton University Press, 2009.

Hammond, N. G. L., and H. H. Scullard, eds. *The Oxford Classical Dictionary,* 2nd ed. Oxford: Clarendon, 1991.

Harding, Brian. *Augustine and Roman Virtue.* New York: Continuum, 2008.

———. "Epistemology and Eudaimonism in Augustine's *Contra Academicos.*" *Augustinian Studies* 37, no. 2 (November 2006): 247–71.

———. "Skepticism, Illumination, and Christianity in Augustine's *Contra Academicos.*" *Augustinian Studies* 34, no. 2 (2003): 197–212.

Harnack, Adolph von. *Augustins Konfessionen.* Geissen: J. Ricker, 1888.

Harrison, Carol. *Augustine: Christian Truth and Fractured Humanity.* Oxford: Oxford University Press, 2000.

———. *Rethinking Augustine's Early Theology: An Argument for Continuity.* Oxford: Oxford University Press, 2008.

Hefferman, Jeanne Marie. "The Nature and Origin of Political Authority in Augustine and Aquinas." Master's thesis, University of Notre Dame, 1995.

Heil, J. "Augustine's Attack on Skepticism: The Contra Academicos." *Harvard Theological Review* 65, no. 1 (1972): 99–116.

———. "Doubts About Skepticism." *Philosophical Studies* 51, no. 1 (1987): 1–17.

Henry, Paul. *Plotin et l'Occident.* Louvain: Spicilegium Sacrum Lovaniense, 1934.

Herodotus. *The Histories.*

Hesiod. *Theogony.*

Heßbrüggen-Walter, Stefan. "Augustine's Critique of Dialectic: Between Ambrose and the Arians." In *Augustine and the Disciplines: From Cassiciacum to* Confession, edited by Karla Pollman and Mark Vessey, 184–205. Oxford: Oxford University Press, 2007.

Heyking, John von. *Augustine and Politics as Longing in the World.* Columbia: University of Missouri Press, 2001.

Hirsch, James E. *Shakespeare and the History of Soliloquies.* Madison, NJ: Fairleigh Dickinson University Press, 2003.

Holt, Laura. "Tolle, Scribe: Augustine at Cassiciacum." PhD diss., University of Notre Dame, 1999.

———. "Wisdom's Teacher: Augustine at Cassiciacum." *Augustinian Studies* 29, no. 2 (1998): 47–60.

Holte, Ragnar. "Monica, 'the Philosopher.'" *Augustinus* 39 (1994): 293–316.

Homer. *The Iliad.*

———. *The Odyssey.*

Horace. *The Art of Poetry (Ars poetica).*

———. *Satires (Satirae).*

Hösle, Vittorio. *The Philosophical Dialogue: A Poetics and a Hermeneutics.* Translated by Steven Rendall. Notre Dame: University of Notre Dame Press, 2013.

Isidore of Seville. *Differentiae.*

Jackson, M. G. St. A. "Augustine All at Sea: An Interpretation of the Opening Paragraphs of *De beata vita*." In *Studia Patristica* 18, no. 4, edited by Elizabeth A. Livingston, 71–77. Louvain: Peeters, 1990.

Jaki, Stanley. *Science and Creation: From Eternal Cycles to an Oscillating Universe.* Edinburgh: Scottish Academic Press, 1974.

Janowski, Zbigniew. *Augustinian-Cartesian Index.* South Bend, IN: St. Augustine's Press, 2004.

Jerome. *Epistle* 70.2.

John Chrysostom. *Homilies.*

Jolivet, R., trans. *Dialogues philosophiques. I. Problèmes fondamentaux. Contra Academicos, De Beata Vita, De Ordine.* Volume. 4 of *Œuvres de Saint Augustin.* Paris: Desclée de Brouwer et Cie, 1948.

Jowett, Benjamin, and J. Harward, trans. *The Dialogues of Plato and the Seventh Letter.* Volume 7 of *Great Books of the Western World.* Edited by Robert M. Hutchins and Mortimer J. Adler. London: Encyclopaedia Britannica, 1952.

Juvenal. *Satires (Satyricon).*

Kamimura, Naoki. "Self-Knowledge and the Disciplines '*in vita*' in Augustine's *De ordine*." *Patristica*, Suppl. vol. 2 (2006): 76–96.

Kavanagh, Denis J., trans. *Answer to Skeptics.* In *The Writings of St. Augustine.* Volume 1 of *The Fathers of the Church Series*, 103–225. New York: Cima, 1948.

Kenyon, Erik. *Augustine and the Dialogue.* Cambridge: Cambridge University Press, 2018.

———. "The Order of Augustine's Cassiciacum Dialogues." *Augustinian Studies* 42, no. 2 (2011): 173–88.

Kevane, Eugene. *Augustine the Educator: A Study in the Fundamentals of Christian Formation*. Westminster, MD: Newman, 1954.

———. "Christian Philosophy: The Intellectual Side of Augustine's Conversion." *Augustinian Studies* 17 (1986): 47–83.

King, Peter, trans. *Augustine: Against the Academicians and The Teacher*. Indianapolis, IN: Hackett, 1995.

Kirwan, Christopher. "Augustine Against the Skeptics." In *The Skeptical Tradition*, edited by Myles Burnyeat, 205–23. Berkeley: University of California Press, 1983.

Klingshirn, William E. "Divination and the Disciplines of Knowledge According to Augustine." In *Augustine and the Disciplines: From Cassiciacum to Confessions*, edited by Karla Pollman and Mark Vessey, 113–40. Oxford: Oxford University Press, 2007.

Kries, Douglas. "Augustine as Defender and Critic of Leo Strauss's Esotericism Thesis." *Proceedings of the ACPA* 83 (2009): 241–52.

Kuritz, Paul. *The Making of Theatre History*. Englewood Cliffs, NJ: Prentice-Hall 1988.

Labriolle, Pierre de, trans. *Dialogues philosophiques. II. Dieu et l'âme. Soliloques, De Immortalitate Animae, De Quantitate Animae*. Volume 5 of *Œuvres de saint Augustin*. Paris: Desclée de Brouwer et Cie, 1948.

Lacey, Thomas. *Nature, Miracle, and Sin: A Study of St. Augustine's Conception of the Natural Order*. New York: Longman, Green, 1916.

Lactantius. *Divine Institutes (Divinae institutiones)*.

Laertes, Diogenes. *Lives of Eminent Philosophers (Bioi kai gnōmai tōn en philosophia eudokimēsantōn)*.

Lawrence, Caroline. *The Beggar of Volubilis*. London: Orion, 2007.

Leake, James. "Lesser Hippias [or, On the Lie]." In *The Roots of Political Philosophy*, edited by Thomas L. Pangle, 281–99. Ithaca, NY: Cornell University Press, 1987.

Levin, Susan B. *The Ancient Quarrel Between Philosophy and Poetry Revisited: Plato and the Greek Literary Tradition*. Oxford: Oxford University Press, 2001.

Lewis, C. S. *The Problem of Pain*. London: Centenary, 1940.

Littlewood, A. R. "Ancient Literary Evidence for Pleasure Gardens of Roman Country Villas." In *Ancient Roman Villa Gardens*, edited by E. B. MacDougall, 9–30. Dumbarton Oaks Colloquium on the History of Landscape Architecture, Book 10. Washington, DC: Dumbarton Oaks Research Library and Collection, 1987.

Livy. *History of Rome (Ab urbe condita)*.

Lonergan, Bernard J. F. *Insight: An Inquiry into Human Understanding*. San Francisco: Harper & Row, 1978.

———. *Method in Theology*. New York: Seabury, 1979.

Loriaux, M. "The Realists and Saint Augustine: Skepticism, Psychology, and Moral Action in International Relations Thought." *International Studies Quarterly* 36, no. 4 (1992): 401–20.

Lucian. *On Pantomime (Peri orcheseos)*.

———. *The Sale of Lives (Biōn Prasis)*.

———. *Symposium (Symposion ē Lapithai)*.

Lucretius. *On the Nature of Things (De rerum natura)*.

Macrobius. *Commentary on the Dream of Scipio (Commentarius in somnium Scipionis)*.

———. *Saturnalia*.

Madec, Goulven. "Cassiciacum." *Revue des Études Augustiniennes* 32 (1986): 207–31.

———. "Connaissance de Dieu et action de graces. Essai sur les citations de l'Epître aux Romains, 1, 18–25." *Revue des Études Augustiniennes* 2 (1962): 273–309.

———. *Introduction aux 'Révisions' et à la lecture des Œuvres de saint Augustin*. Paris: Études Augustiniennes, 1996.

———. "The Notion of Philosophical Augustinianism: An Attempt at Clarification." *Mediaevalia* 4 (1978): 125–46.

———. *Saint Augustin et la philosophie*. Paris: Études Augustiniennes, 1996.

Mallard, William. "The Incarnation in Augustine's Conversion." *Recherches Augustiniennes* 15 (1989): 80–98.

Mandouze, André. *L'aventure de la raison et de la grace*. Paris: Études Augustiniennes, 1968.

Manilius, Marcus. *Astronomica*.

Marrou, H. I. *Saint Augustin et la fin de la culture antique*. 2nd ed. Paris: E. de Boccard, 1949.

Martial. *Epigrams (Epigramma)*.

Maximus, Valerius. *Memorable Deeds and Sayings (Factorum ac dictorum memorabilium libri IX)*.

McWilliam, Joanne. "The Cassiciacum Autobiography." In *Studia Patristica* 18, no. 4, 14–43. Louvain: Peeters, 1990.

Mekler, Siegfried, ed. *Academicorum philosophorum index Herculanensis.* Berlin: Weidmannos, 1902.

Melzer, Arthur. *Philosophy Between the Lines: The Lost History of Esoteric Writing.* Chicago: University of Chicago Press, 2014.

Miner, Robert. "Augustinian Recollection." *Augustinian Studies* 38, no. 2 (2007): 435–50.

Minucius Felix. *Octavius.*

Missale Romanum: Editio Typica 1962. Vatican City: Libreria Editrice Vaticana, 2007.

Mosher, David L. "The Argument of Augustine's *Contra Academicos.*" *Augustinian Studies* 12 (1981): 89–113.

Mourant, John A. "Augustine and the Academics." *Recherches Augustiniennes* 4 (1966): 67–96.

———. "The Emergence of a Christian Philosophy in the Dialogues of Augustine." *Augustinian Studies* 1 (1970): 70–88.

Müller, C. F. W., ed. *M. Tulli Ciceronis Scripta quae Manserunt Omnia*, 4:3. Leipzig: Teubner, 1898.

Nash, R. H. "Some Philosophic Sources of Augustine's Illumination Theory." *Augustinian Studies* 2 (1971): 47–66.

Neiman, Alven Michael. "The Arguments of Augustine's 'Contra Academicos.' " *Modern Schoolman* 59 (May 1982): 255–80.

———. "Augustine's Philosophizing Person: The View at Cassiciacum." *New Scholasticism* 58, no. 2 (Spring 1984): 236–55.

Newman, John Henry. *The Idea of a University.* Notre Dame: University of Notre Dame Press, 1982.

Nicgorski, Walter. *Cicero's Skepticism and His Recovery of Political Philosophy.* New York: Palgrave Macmillan, 2016.

O'Connell, J. B., ed. *The Roman Martyrology.* Westminster, MD: Newman, 1962.

O'Connell, Robert. *Art and the Christian Intelligence in St. Augustine.* Cambridge, MA: Harvard University Press, 1978.

———. "Enneads VI, 4–5, in the Works of St. Augustine." *Revue des Études Augustiniennes* 9 (1963): 1–39.

———. "The Enneads and St. Augustine's Image of Happiness." *Vigiliae Christianae* 17, no. 3 (September 1994): 129–64.

———. "On Augustine's 'First Conversion': Factus erectior (*de beata vita 4*)." *Augustinian Studies* 17 (1986): 15–29.

———. *Soundings in St. Augustine's Imagination.* New York: Fordham University Press, 1994.

———. *St. Augustine's Early Theory of Man, A.D. 386–391.* Cambridge, MA: Harvard University Press, 1968.

———. *St. Augustine's Platonism.* Villanova, PA: Augustinian Institute, 1984.

———. "The Visage of Philosophy at Cassiciacum." *Augustinian Studies* 25 (1994): 65–76.

O'Daly, Gerard. *Augustine's Philosophy of Mind.* Berkeley: University of California Press, 1987.

———. "Did St. Augustine Ever Believe in the Soul's Pre-existence?" *Augustinian Studies* 5 (1974): 227–35.

———. "Memory in Plotinus and Two Early Texts of St. Augustine." In *Platonism Pagan and Christian: Studies in Plotinus and Augustine,* 462–69. Aldershot: Ashgate, 2001.

———. "The Response to Skepticism and the Mechanisms of Cognition." In *The Cambridge Companion to Augustine,* edited by Elenore Stump and Norman Kretzman, 159–70. Cambridge: Cambridge University Press, 2006.

O'Donnell, James D. *Augustine Confessions.* 3 vols. Oxford: Clarendon, 1992.

O'Donovan, Oliver. *"Usus* and *Fruitio* in Augustine, *De Doctrina,* I." *Journal of Theological Studies* 33, no. 2 (1982): 361–97.

O'Ferrall, Margaret More. "Monica: A Reconsideration." *Recherches Augustiniennes* 10 (1974): 23–43.

Ohlmann, Desiderius. *De Sancti Augustini dialogis in Cassiciaco scriptis.* Strassburg: Argentorati, 1897.

Oliver, Simon. *Philosophy, God and Motion.* Abingdon: Routledge, 2005.

O'Meara, John J. "The Historicity of the Early Dialogues." *Vigiliae Christianae* 5, no. 1 (1951): 150–78.

———. "Plotinus and Augustine: Exegesis of 'Contra Academicos II Point 5." *Revue Internationale de Philosophie* 24 (1970): 321–37.

———. *Porphyry's Philosophy from Oracles in Eusebius's* Praeparatio evangelica *and Augustine's Dialogues of Cassiciacum.* Paris: Études Augustiniennes, 1969.

———. "Prolegomena to the Contra Academicos of St. Augustine." Thesis, University of Oxford, 1944.

———. *St. Augustine: Against the Academics.* Volume 12 of *Ancient Christian Writers.* Edited by Johannes Quasten and Joseph Plumpe. Westminster, MD: Newman, 1950.

———. *The Young Augustine: The Growth of St. Augustine's Mind Up to His Conversion.* Staten Island, NY: St. Paul, 1965.

Origen. *Against Celsus* (*Contra Celsum*).

———. *On First Principles* (*De principiis*).

Ovid. *Lamentations* (*Tristia*).

———. *The Loves* (*Amores*).

———. *Metamorphoses.*

Paffenroth, Kim, trans. *Soliloquies: Augustine's Interior Dialogue.* Hyde Park, NY: New City Press, 2000.

Parry, Richard. "Ancient Ethical Theory." Stanford Encyclopedia of Philosophy, http://plato.stanford.edu/entries/ethics-ancient/, last revised August 13, 2014.

Pascal, Blaise. *Pensées.* Translated by A. J. Krailsheimer. London: Penguin, 1966.

Paulinus of Nola. *The Life of Ambrose* (*Vita Ambrosii*).

Petronius. *Satyricon.*

Plato. *Alcibiades I.* All translations of Plato are from Jowett and Harward, unless otherwise noted.

———. *Apology.*

———. *Cratylus.*

———. *Euthyphro.*

———. *Gorgias.*

———. *Laws.*

———. *Lesser Hippias.* Translations from Leake, "Lesser Hippias."

———. *Letters.*

———. *Meno.*

———. *Parmenides.*

———. *Phaedo.*

———. *Phaedrus.*

———. *Republic.* Translations from Bloom, Allan. *The Republic of Plato.* New York: Basic Books, 1968.

———. *Symposium.*

———. *Theaetetus.*

———. *Timaeus.*

Plautus. *The Brothers Menaechmus* (*Menaechmi*).

———. *The Persian* (*Persa*).

Pliny. *Natural History* (*Naturalis historia*).

Plotinus. *Enneads.* Translations from *The Six Enneads.* Translated by Stephen MacKenna and B. S. Page. Whitefish, MT: Kessinger, 2004.

Plutarch. *Lives* (*Bioi Parallēloi*).

Pollman, Karla, and Mark Vessey, eds. *Augustine and the Disciplines: From Cassiciacum to Confessions.* Oxford: Oxford University Press, 2005.

Pollux. *Onomasticon.*

Porphyry. *Against the Christians (Adversus Christianos).*

——. *Letter to Anebo (Epistula ad Anebonem).*

——. *Letter to Marcella (Epistula ad Marcellam).*

——. *Life of Plotinus (Vita Plotini).*

——. *Thoughts Leading to the Intelligibles (Sententiae ad intelligibilia ducentes).*

Possidius. *Index of the Works of Saint Augustine (Indiculum operum s. Augustini).*

Proclus. *Commentary on Plato's Timaeus (In Platonis Timaeum commentaria).*

——. *Elements of Theology (Institutio theologica).*

Pseudo-Cicero. *Rhetoric for Herennius (Rhetorica ad Herennium).*

Pucci, Joseph. *Augustine's Virgilian Retreat: Reading the Auctores at Cassiciacum.* Toronto: Pontifical Institute of Mediaeval Studies, 2014.

Puchner, Martin. *The Drama of Ideas: Platonic Provocations in Theatre and Philosophy.* Oxford: Oxford University Press, 2010.

Quintilian. *Minor Declamations (Declamationes minores).*

——. *Oratorical Instruction (Institutio oratoria).*

Ratzinger, Joseph. *On the Way to Jesus Christ.* Translated by Michael J. Miller. San Francisco: Ignatius Press, 2005.

Rist, John M. *Augustine: Ancient Thought Baptized.* Cambridge: Cambridge University Press, 1994.

——. "Plotinus and Augustine on Evil." In *Atti del Convegno Internazionale Sul Tema: Plotino e il Neoplatonismo in Oriente e in Occidente,* 495–508. Roma: Accademia Nazionale dei Lincei, 1974.

——. "Plotinus and Christian Philosophy." In *Cambridge Companion to Plotinus,* edited by Lloyd P. Gerson, 386–413. Cambridge: Cambridge University Press, 1996.

Roberts, David E. "Augustine's Earliest Writings." *Journal of Religion* 33, no. 3 (1953): 161–81.

Rombs, Ronnie, ed. *Saint Augustine and the Fall of the Soul: Beyond O'Connell and His Critics.* Washington, DC: Catholic University of America Press, 2006.

Rossiter, Jeremy. "Convivium and Villa in Late Antiquity." In *Dining in a Classical Context,* edited by William Slater, 199–214. Ann Arbor: University of Michigan Press, 1991.

Roy, Olivier du. *L'intelligence de la foi en la trinité selon saint Augustin: genèse de sa théologie trinitaire jusqu'en 391.* Paris: Études Augustiniennes, 1966.

Russell, Robert P. "Cicero's Hortensius and the Problem of Riches in Saint Augustine." *Augustinian Studies* 7 (1976): 59–69.

———, trans. *Divine Providence and the Problem of Evil.* New York: Cosmopolitan Science and Art Service, 1942.

Sallust. *Catiline (De conjuratione Catilinae or Bellum Catilinae).*

Schofiled, Malcolm. "Academic Epistemology." In *Cambridge History of Hellenistic Philosophy*, edited by Keimpe Algra, Jonathan Barnes, Jaap Mansfield, and Malcolm Schofield, 323–51. Cambridge: Cambridge University Press, 1999.

Schopp, Ludwig, trans. *The Happy Life.* In *The Writings of St. Augustine.* Volume 1 of *The Fathers of the Church Series.* New York: Cima, 1948.

Schumacher, Lydia. "The 'Theo-Logic' of Augustine's Theory of Knowledge by Divine Illumination." *Augustinian Studies* 41, no. 2 (2011): 375–99.

Seneca. *Epistles (Epistulae).*

———. *On Clemency (De clementia).*

———. *On the Constancy of the Wise Man (De constantia sapientis).*

———. *On the Happy Life (De vita beata).*

———. *To Helvia on Consolation (De consolatione ad Helviam matrem).*

Servius. *Commentary on the Aeneid of Vergil (In Aeneidem).*

———. *Commentary on the Eclogues of Vergil (In Eclogis).*

Sextus Empiricus. *Against the Mathematicians (Adversos Mathematicos).*

———. *Outlines of Pyrrhonism (Pyrrhōneioi hypotypōseis).* Translations from *The Skeptic Way: Sextus Empiricus's Outlines of Pyrrhonism.* Translated by Benson Mates. Oxford: Oxford University Press, 1996.

Seyffert, Oskar. "Mimus." In *Dictionary of Classical Antiquities*, edited by Henry Nettleship and J. E. Sandys, 393. New York: Meridian, 1957.

———. "Pantomimus," In *Dictionary of Classical Antiquities*, edited by Henry Nettleship and J. E. Sandys, 457. New York: Meridian, 1957.

Smalbrugge, Matthias S. "L'argumentation probabiliste d'Augustin." *Revue des Études Augustiniennes* 32 (1986): 41–55.

Smith, James K. A. "Staging the Incarnation: Revisioning Augustine's Critique of Theatre." *Literature and Theology* 15, no. 2 (June 2001): 123–39.

Sonny, A. "Neue Sprichtvörter und sprichwörtliche. Redensarten der Römer." In *Archiv für lateinische lexicographie* 8, 483–94. Leipzig: Teubner, 1893.

Sophocles. *Oedipus Tyrannus.* Translations from *The Complete Plays of Sophocles.* Translated by Sir Richard Claverhouse. New York: Bantam Classics, 1991.

Southern, Pat, and Karen R. Dixon. *The Late Roman Army.* New Haven: Yale University Press, 1996.

Spano, John. "Augustine's *Contra Academicos* as a Response to Cicero's *Academica.*" PhD diss., Baylor University, 2013.

Spitzer, Robert. "The Curious Metaphysics of Dr. Stephen Hawking." CERC, Catholic Education Research Center. September 3, 2010, Magis Institute. https://www.catholiceducation.org/en/science/faith-and-science/the-curious-metaphysics-of-dr-stephen-hawking.html.

Steppat, Michael P. *Die Schola von Cassiciacum: Augustins 'De ordine.'* Frankfurt: Bock and Herchen, 1980.

Statius. *The Woods (Silvae)*.

Stock, Brian. *Augustine's Inner Dialogue: The Philosophical Soliloquy in Late Antiquity.* Cambridge: Cambridge University Press, 2010.

———. *Augustine the Reader: Meditation, Self-Knowledge, and the Ethics of Interpretation.* Cambridge, MA: Harvard University Press, 1996.

Strauss, Leo. *City and Man.* Chicago: Rand McNally, 1964.

———. "Exoteric Teaching." In *The Rebirth of Classical Political Rationalism: An Introduction to the Thought of Leo Strauss*, edited by Thomas L. Pangle, 63–71. Chicago: University of Chicago Press, 1989.

———. "On a Forgotten Kind of Writing." In *What Is Political Philosophy?*, 221–32. Glencoe, IL: Free Press, 1959.

———. *Persecution and the Art of Writing.* Glencoe, IL: Free Press, 1952.

Syrianus. *Commentary on Aristotle's Metaphysics (In Aristotelis Metaphysica commentaria)*.

Tacitus. *A Dialogue on Orators (Dialogus de oratoribus)*.

———. *Histories (Historiae)*.

Taylor, Rabun. *The Moral Mirror of Roman Art.* Cambridge: Cambridge University Press, 2008.

Terence. *The Eunuch (Eunuchus)*.

———. *Lady of Andros (Andria)*.

———. *The Mother-in-Law (Hecyra)*.

———. *Phormio.*

———. *Self-Tormentor (Heauton Timorumenos)*.

Tertullian. *On the Spectacles (De spectaculis)*.

TeSelle, Eugene. *Augustine the Theologian.* London: Burns and Oates, 1970.

Teske, Roland J. "Augustine of Hippo on Seeing with the Eyes of the Mind." In *Ambiguity in Western Thought*, edited by Craig J. N. de Paulo, Patrick Messina, and Marc Stier, 72–87 and 221–26. New York: Peter Lang, 2005.

———. "Augustine's Third Conversion: A Case for Discontinuity." In *Proceedings of the Jesuit Philosophical Association*, edited by Joseph Koterski. (2007): 19–38.

———, trans. *The Happy Life*. In *Trilogy on Faith and Happiness*, edited by Bonfiace Ramsey, 9–54. Hyde Park, NY: New City Press, 2010.

———. "Heresy and Imagination in St. Augustine." *Studia Patristica*27 (1991): 400–404.

———. "Saint Augustine as Philosopher: The Birth of Christian Metaphysics." *Augustinian Studies* 23 (1992): 7–32.

———. "St. Augustine's Epistula X: Another Look at 'Deificari in otio.' " *Augustinianum* 32 (1992): 289–99.

———. *To Know God and the Soul: Essays on the Thought of Saint Augustine*. Washington, DC: Catholic University of America Press, 2008.

Testard, Maurice. *Augustin et Cicéron*. Paris: Études Augustiniennes, 1958.

———. "Cicero." In *Augustinus-Lexikon*, Volume 1, edited by Cornelius Mayer, 916–18. Basel: Schwabe, 1994.

Theiler, Willy. *Porphyrios und Augustin*. Halle: Niemeyer, 1933.

Thomas Aquinas. *Commentary on Boethius'* De Trinitate (*Expositio super librum Boethii De Trinitate*)

———. *Summa Contra Gentiles*

———. *Summa Theologiae*.

Thomas More. A *Dialogue Concerning Heresies*. Volume 6, Part I, of the *Complete Works of St. Thomas More*, edited by Thomas M. C. Lawler, Germain Marc Hadour, and Richard C. Marius. New Haven: Yale University Press, 1981.

Tkacz, Michael W. "A Designer Universe: Thomas Aquinas on Chance and Design in the Cosmos." Unpublished lecture, 2005 Aquinas Lecture at Thomas Aquinas College.

Tibullus. *Elegies* (*Elegiae*).

Tocqueville, Alexis de. *Democracy in America*. Translated by George Lawrence. Garden City, NY: Anchor, 1969.

Topping, Ryan N. S. *Happiness and Wisdom: Augustine's Early Theology of Education*. Washington, DC: Catholic University of America Press, 2012.

Torchia, Joseph N. *Creatio ex nihilo and the Theology of St. Augustine/The Anti-Manichean Polemic and Beyond*. New York: Peter Lang, 1999.

———. "The Significance of *Ordo* in St. Augustine's Moral Theory." In *Augustine: Presbyter Factus Sum*, 263–78. Edited by J. T. Lienhard, E. C. Muller, and R. J. Teske. New York: Peter Lang, 1993.

Tornau, Christian. "*Ratio in subjecto?* The Sources of Augustine's Proof for the Immortality of the Soul in the *Soliloquia* and Its Defense in *De immortalitate animae*." *Phronesis* 62 (2017): 319–54.

Tourscher, Francis E., trans. *Saint Augustine: De Beata Vita, De Immortalitate Animae*. Philadelphia: Peter Reilly, 1937.

Trout, Dennis E. "Augustine at Cassiciacum: *Otium Honestum* and the Social Dimensions of Conversion." *Vigiliae Christianae* 42 (1988): 132–46.

Ulpian. Quoted in the *Digest* (*Digesta Justiniani*).

Valentin, Pierre. "Un pretreptique conserve de l'antiquité: le '*Contra Academicos*' de Saint Augustin." *Revue des Sciences Religieuses* 43, no. 1 (1969): 1–26.

Van der Meeren, Sophie. "La sagesse 'droit chemin de la vie': une métaphore du *Contra Academicos* relue à la lumière du protreptique philosophique." *Revue des Études Augustiniennes* 53 (2007): 81–111.

Van Fleteren, Frederick E. "Authority and Reason, Faith and Understanding in the Thought of St. Augustine." *Augustinian Studies* 4 (1973): 33–71.

———. "The Cassiciacum Dialogues and Augustine's Ascents at Milan." *Mediaevalia* 4 (1978): 159–82.

Van Slyke, Daniel G. "The Order of Exorcist in the Latin Patristic Period: Reconsidered in Light of Martin of Tours." *Ephemerides Liturgicae* 123 (2009): 357–79.

Varro, Marcus Terentius. *On Agricultural Topics* (*De re rustica*).

———. *On the Latin Language* (*De lingua Latina*).

———. *On the Usefulness of the Word* (*De utilitate sermonis*). Fragments from Wilmanns, Augustus. *De M. Terenti Varronis libris grammaticis*. Rhein: Friedrich-Wilhelm-University, 1863.

———. *Satura Menippea* 144. From *Petronii Satirae et Liber Priapeorum*, edited by Franciscus Buecheler, 177. Berlin: Weidmann, 1882.

Vergil. *Aeneid*.

———. *Eclogues*.

———. *Georgics*.

Vessey, Mark. "Introduction" to *Augustine and the Disciplines: From Cassiciacum to Confessions*, edited by Karla Pollman and Mark Vessey, 1–21. Oxford: Oxford University Press, 2007.

Victorinus, Marius. *Against Arius* (*Adversus Arium*).

———. *Commentary on Ephesians* (*In Epistolam Pauli ad Ephesios*).

———. *Grammar* (*Ars Grammatica*).

———. *Hymns* (*Hymni*).

———. *Letter to Candidus* (*Ad Candidum*).

Vitruvius. *The Ten Books on Architecture* (*De architectura*).

Voegelin, Eric. *Autobiographical Reflections*. Baton Rouge: Louisiana State University Press, 1989.

Watson, Gerard, trans. *Soliloquies and Immortality of the Soul*. Warminster: Aris & Phillips, 1990.

West, M. L. *The Orphic Poems*. New York: Oxford University Press, 1983.

Wetzel, James. *Augustine and the Limits of Virtue*. Cambridge: Cambridge University Press, 1992.

Wilder, Thornton. *The Bridge of San Luis Rey*. New York: Perennial Classics, 1986. First published 1927.

Wilmanns, G. *Inscriptiones Africae Latinae*. Volume 8 of *Corpus inscriptionum latinarum.*, edited by Theodor Mommsen. Berlin: Reimerum, 1881.

Xenophon. *Memorabilia.*

INDEX